African and African American Images in Newbery Award Winning Titles

Progress in Portrayals

Binnie Tate Wilkin

THE SCARECROW PRESS, INC.
Lanham • Toronto • Plymouth, UK
2009

Published by Scarecrow Press, Inc.
A wholly owned subsidiary of The Rowman & Littlefield Publishing Group, Inc.
4501 Forbes Boulevard, Suite 200, Lanham, Maryland 20706
http://www.scarecrowpress.com

Estover Road, Plymouth PL6 7PY, United Kingdom

British Library Cataloguing in Publication Information Available

Library of Congress Cataloging-in-Publication Data

Wilkin, Binnie Tate, 1933–
    African and African American images in Newbery award winning titles :
progress in portrayals / Binnie Tate Wilkin.
        p. cm.
    Includes bibliographical references and index.
    ISBN 978-0-8108-6959-2 (pbk. : alk. paper) — ISBN 978-0-8108-6960-8
(ebook)
    1. Children's literature—History and criticism. 2. African Americans in
literature. 3. Africans in literature. 4. Newbery Medal. 5. Africa—In
literature. I. Title.
PN1009.5.A47W55 2009
810.9'352996073—dc22

                                                            2009017726

⊗ ™ The paper used in this publication meets the minimum requirements of
American National Standard for Information Sciences—Permanence of Paper
for Printed Library Materials, ANSI/NISO Z39.48-1992.

Printed in the United States of America

To *all* the children of the world

Contents

Foreword

NOT-SO-SUBTLE IMAGES of Blacks as ignorant; always the servant; never in charge of anything (not themselves, their families, or their tempers); and unable to achieve because they have inherent deficits are the legacies that have been left our children in vehicles that are supposed to move them ahead in life—books. Some may ponder, "What difference does it make? They are just stories . . . fiction . . . harmless." The old sticks-and-stones adage that they are "just words" and not aimed at anyone may seem to apply. The problem, however, is that books are not just words. They provide the first of many models that children will begin to integrate as they attempt to find their way in the world, to form their self-image, and to build their feelings of self worth. Books hold knowledge, after all! When one is consistently presented with negative images from a valued source, what else could one believe? How are Black children supposed to be empowered to achieve when they are consistently being told in insidious, subliminal ways that they "can't," or at least, aren't supposed to, and that the successful African American is the exception to the rule?

Drawing attention to race portrayals of people of color is a controversial issue in many fields. In a 2008 address to the American Psychological Association, Dr. Hazel Rose Markus stated, "Many Americans feel that paying attention to ethnic and racial differences is at odds with our ideals of individual equality and our belief that, at the end of the day, people are people." Others may argue, "Why the emphasis on portraying people of color? I am trying to write literature that is color-blind." While that sounds positive in theory, the truth is that attempts at color blindness further exacerbate the problem. We live in a world where race matters. People's worldviews are based on their identities, and one's personal identity is heavily influenced by definitions of race and culture. By failing to acknowledge race, the experiences that come with being a person of color are discounted. Pretending that the world can be color-blind doesn't make it so. Excluding images of racial/cultural differences in literature doesn't make it inclusive but makes it insensitive at best and harmful at its worst.

Children are not likely to question what they consider reliable sources. They read that princesses exist and that Santa will be down the chimney on December twenty-fifth and they believe that is so. This fact integration is problematic when these same children are presented with images in books that lead them to believe negative things about themselves and others. How many books with the absence of minority characters does it take to make a child believe that they don't matter—that they are invisible? How many negative portrayals of people with the same racial background does it take to make a child believe that there is something deficient in those people that will not change?

Empowerment theory tells us that children need to believe that they have within them the ability to succeed. They need to be given messages relaying that they can control their futures. They must develop positive self-images. How does that happen when they are bombarded with messages to the contrary? Children use information gathered from sources like books to shape their perceptions of the world and their roles in it. This perception forms their reality and in many ways dictates the steps they will take in the future. It is the responsibility of authors, teachers, and parents to ensure that children are provided with positive images so perceptions developed tell them that they are worthy of love, that they can achieve, and that they aren't invisible.

The practice of either not portraying or negatively portraying African Americans in literature not only affects Black children but also negatively affects their peers. It gives other children a skewed view of African American people and culture and may cause confusion and other problems as they grow to interact with African American peers and authority figures in the future. When positive images of African Americans or other minorities are absent from literature, it deprives children of the images they need in order to appreciate others as well as themselves. In his 1987 poem "Freedom's Child," Bill Martin Jr. further illustrates this when he says, "We need all the different kinds of people we can find, to make freedom's dream come true, so as I learn to like the differences in me, I learn to like the differences in you."

In his writings, noted Black psychologist Frantz Fanon asserts that the oppression of Blacks during and following the Middle Passage led to cultural alienation. This alienation continues to be perpetuated by the absence of positive images in media of all types. Fanon describes "intrusion into the psyche" that occurs from prolonged oppression coupled with an obliteration of the culture, language, and history of the oppressed group. It is an intrusion into the psyche that we must combat. It causes some children to believe they are subordinate to the dominant culture and must disconnect themselves from their own culture and ethnicity in order to succeed. These children do not want to be Black. They have been presented so many negative images that they come to believe that being Black is bad. They grow into adults who cling to the majority culture and condemn their own people to avoid being reminded that they are African American and as such are not supposed to succeed. We cannot continue to allow children to grow up in environments that subliminally oppress them or those that allow them to believe they must deny who they are in order to be accepted and to achieve.

Having a strong cultural identity is critical to overall development. It is important that children have the tools available to them in a multitude of venues to develop such identities. They should be embraced with positive images of people who look like them at home and in the media. To pretend that having a racial identity is unimportant is fantasy at its worst. In his memoir, *Colored People*, Henry Louis Gates Jr. illustrates this point by saying, "Part of me admires those people who say with a straight face that they have transcended any attachment to a particular community or group . . . but I always want to run around them to see what holds them up." Don't be mistaken. The message is not that one's sole focus should be on ethnic identity. We are certainly more than our race, but to neglect this important construct is to deny the very essence of self. A person without racial identity is missing an essential piece of himself. It is impossible to develop a positive sense of one's place in the world without developing knowledge about and an appreciation for your ethnic group. It has often been said they you must know where you came from to know where you are going. Similarly, a child who grows up without a positive sense of racial identity may be lost.

Binnie Tate Wilkin's book *African and African American Images in Newbery Award Winning Titles* highlights important issues about literature at a time when we need it most. We want to believe that racism is no longer a problem and that we can assume the playing field is now equal. At this period in history when we have just elected the first African American president of the United States, it is important that we do not become complacent. Certainly, we have come a long way from early American literature, with the only characters of color being slaves or servants, and progress has been seen in children's literature over the past twenty years. We have begun to show the way toward making multicultural representations and images of inclusion the rule, but to quote Robert Frost, we still have "miles to go before [we] sleep." We must continue to critically examine the images being promulgated to our youth and hold authors accountable for the legacy that they are leaving our children. It is no longer enough to mention Blacks as peripheral characters. Black people are integral to the history and progress of America. For the sake of our children, Black characters must be integral to American stories.

Emily L. Streeter, Psy.D.
Honolulu, Hawaii

Acknowledgments

My sincere thanks to the staff of the Los Angeles City Library's Children Literature Department, especially Diane Olivo-Posner, for their gracious assistance. Thanks to Gladys Cole and all others who assisted me in getting this task completed.

Introduction

DURING MY YEARS AS A PROFESSIONAL LIBRARIAN, library school lecturer, consultant, and storyteller, my primary area of specialty was children's services and materials. Believing that education, including that received through books, could help young people survive in a complex world, I wrote *Survival Themes in Literature for Children and Young People*, published in 1978 by Scarecrow Press, followed by another edition in 1993. In 2007, at the First National Conference of Librarians of Color, my paper "What Progress? African and African American Images in the Newbery Award, 1990–2007" was presented. Those attending expressed an interest in this material and suggested that more be written. This manuscript has been expanded to survey *all titles* from the beginning of the Newbery Award to present.

Purposes for this exploration are as follows:

- To examine books receiving the nation's top award for children's books for images of Africans and African Americans;
- To evaluate those materials containing such images;
- To offer opinions about the presentation of African American images in the context of societal events and views;
- To inform teachers, librarians, parents, counselors, and so forth about these images, some of which are subtle and obscure; and

- To participate in continuing discussions and dialogues regarding the perpetuation of racial prejudice.

Evaluations are offered for guidance and nothing more. There is no intention here to censor.

PROCESS

All titles receiving the Newbery Award or an honor award from 1922 to 2009 were read or reread and examined for references to persons of African descent. All titles with any mention of Africans or African Americans were noted, not just those that included major characters or those in which the protagonist was of African descent. Books that discussed slavery and other pertinent aspects of history are listed regardless of the presentation of identifiable persons. Any references missed were accidental.

Each title was examined for overall portrayals, racial stereotypes, sensitivity, aesthetic descriptions, language, and historical accuracy. In addition criteria for award selection were considered. Not all Newbery selections are reviewed; materials with African and African American images have been given emphasis and those reviews are listed first. A second list contains ancillary titles and selected titles of cultural interest. The final chapter reviews the remainder of the *winning* titles. Some honor award titles are omitted.

Some books were out of print, but copies were found in public library special collections, colleges, and universities. All seemed to be available for purchase somewhere on the Internet.

Many professional titles reference the Newbery Award, its history, and its background. Information about the award is available from the American Library Association (ala.org). Also available are numerous reviews of all the books. None, however, was found with concentrated attention paid to the subjects discussed herein.

A foreword by Emily L. Streeter, Psy.D., was included to denote the importance of providing young people, in their early years and beyond, with accurate, unbiased, and informed materials.

Background and Analysis

IN A WORLD FACED WITH CONFLICTS based on cultural differences, it seems imperative that all educational factors that could aid in eliminating such problems be examined. Peoples of different religions and skin colors, even in historically similar groups, are involved in tragic killings and genocides. Education that is encompassing and fair could help the young begin to focus on human survival beyond such influences. Although the Internet and popular media are major influences on young minds, books continue to be a major learning factor. Materials promoted as the best of literature often become items of focus and of constant use.

Children rely on parents, teachers, and others to help them navigate and understand their world, while indirectly, purveyors of books, stories, and other media assume responsibility relating to educating and entertaining the young. Institutions established in the "public trust," such as schools and public libraries, are also forces in this process. Child psychologists agree that, in their early years, children begin to form attitudes about class, race, beauty, and other aspects of society. To young children, everything they read and absorb is truth. They learn by rote, example, vicarious experience, and by observation and interaction with adults. Through these methods they also determine what and whom are valued by the adults close to them and by the larger society. Information absorbed while young begins to "shape" the adult a person becomes.

It could be assumed, therefore, that children exposed only to books and media representing one racial and cultural group value only that perspective. Finding security and, sometimes, superiority in such limited and separate visions, children could show resistance and even resentment to learning about others. Racial and cultural turmoil, globally, offers strong evidence that cultural biases inevitably lead to conflict. Moreover, the inability to value those who are different inhibits positive international negotiations. Americans and the rest of the world have shown a chronic inability to deal with Africanness, with people whose color is of darker hues, and with people whose physical and facial features are not similar to those of Europeans. The strength of the European model for beauty has permeated all cultures, causing many to doubt their own physical worthiness.

In his 1903 publication, *The Souls of Black Folks*, W. E. B. Du Bois wrote, "The white man, as well as the Negro, is bound and barred by the color-line, and many a scheme of friendliness and philanthropy, of broad minded sympathy and genuine fellowship has dropped stillborn."[1] Recently, cross-cultural acceptance of popular music, moderately increased portrayals of African Americans on television, and the Internet has helped to partially blur these lines. Statistics reveal, however, that African Americans still populate those communities in dire poverty to excess. African American and Hispanic men represent the majority in the prison population. Schools, neighborhoods, and especially churches are still segregated to a fault.

Many areas of African and African American history remain hidden even as communication has reached a phenomenal pitch with the Internet. Prejudices produced by so-called scientific and social analyses of Africanness still "color" the minds of world populations. Many of these materials were promulgated as a justification for slavery. The effects of these early projections about the basic humanness of a people have been hard to erase, though much progress has been made. Progress in the law combined with the social and economic advancement of many are apparent, while the examination of social norms present a much more complex picture. Racial and cultural intermarriage is on the rise, but there are questions about how to identify the offspring of such mixtures. African American heroes are often those who have reached millionaire status through sports, the media, and other areas of entertainment. Admittedly, worship of media-made heroes is rampant on all fronts, but this particularly affects the aspirations of African American children.

INFLUENCING PUBLISHERS AND BOOK AWARDS

In the 1960s and '70s, attempts were made by African American librarians and others to exert influence on the production of books for children. The consideration of African American authors and the presence of African Americans in children's materials were the focus. Raising the consciousness of publishers and the larger community was the purpose. Increasing positive African and African American images in children's books was the goal. Equally important was focusing attention on stereotyped images presented in past and current offerings. Because of intellectual freedom issues, most complex were the following questions: Would anyone accept responsibility for printing, selling, publicizing, and placing for public reference materials that were in fact pejorative (simpleminded and implicitly racist if not purposely pejorative)? Should such materials be prominently and continually placed in libraries, especially in children's collections? Those voices combined with the social forces of the civil rights movement seemed to have some effect. At least, the issues were brought to the forefront for discussion. Related phenomena emerged in the general community, such as the NAACP's Image Awards, attempting to influence performance areas of media and to counter the major media's refusal to present culturally different images to the world.

During that time, and immediately thereafter, some editors admitted their cultural isolation. Many had little knowledge of the life of African Americans, especially life outside New York City. Some attended programs and discussions of these issues, prevalent for a while, at the American Library Association. Two of the reasons given for excluding African American images were fear that those materials would not sell in the South and the assumption that no African American market worth pursuing existed.

Many issues regarding the presentation of African Americans in literature were discussed. Among them was an apparent syndrome that existed among Caucasian authors in presenting African American characters. It was termed the "suffering servant" syndrome, which appeared to apply particularly to "acceptable" African American male portrayals. In essence, this is the African American character who serves and probably saves a Caucasian person, often a child, and is considered heroic for this reason. One book accused of this syndrome was *The Cay* by Theodore Taylor.[2]

Another problem was the presentation of white characters as always smart, handsome, or pretty while black characters were secondary, ignorant, or almost invisible. The fact that a character was "black" might in some cases be the only descriptor. In the case of *The Cay*, written descriptors presented a West Indian male as looking almost horrific and revolting, while the cover picture represented an "everyman" Black male.

Presentation of language was a problem that had been attacked many years earlier. Augusta Baker, renowned children's literature specialist and storyteller, wrote about her early involvement in challenges to editors in an article titled "Guidelines for Black Books: An Open Letter to Juvenile Editors." She mentions that at one time books were so full of dialect you couldn't understand them and suggests that only regional vernacular is acceptable. She declared that no derogatory terms should be included in children's books unless historically necessary.[3]

Years of relegating African Americans to invisible or negative status have deprived everyone, including African American authors, of adequate descriptive language. For example, "black" is not an appropriate descriptor for all characters. African American authors as well as others are challenged to be inventive in presenting such descriptors. Walter Mosley wrote, "Black people are not all black; they are white people and yellow people, red and brown people who feel the beat of history in their blood, while they witness the barbarism of hierarchy."[4] In the books that have been honored by the Newbery award, there are many characters in European, Spanish, and South American settings referred to simply as "dark," with no reference to whether this means dark in color or simply having dark hair and eyes. The influence of Africa and Africanness in places around the world is often ignored as are many aspects of African history and influence in the United States. Although seldom mentioned, Africans came to America as explorers and servants as well as slaves. As John Hope Franklin, the noted historian, writes, "Thirty Negroes, including Nuflo de Olano were with Balboa when he discovered the Pacific Ocean,"[5] and "Africans were in Europe in considerable numbers in the seventeenth century."[6] Little recognition of their presence is found in the children's materials documenting this period. Among Newbery Award winners, *Amos Fortune* is one of the few titles acknowledging the presence of free Africans in America during the period of slavery. According to Franklin, statistical records show their presence both north and south. Some accumulated substantial property for the times.[7]

Children's literature features a lot of materials about the First Nations and tribal groups of the United States. Few approach the matter of Africans having been enslaved and/or adopted by tribal groups. Through pictures and information in William Katz's book *Black Indians, A Hidden Heritage*, published in 1986, some of this lost information was recovered.[8]

During the turbulent times of the '60s and '70s, several African American authors of children's books entered the market, partially due to advocacy by librarians. The Council on Interracial Books' publication edited by Brad Chambers and titled *Bulletin of Interracial Books for Children* became one of the prominent publications airing issues of racism and multiculturalism. The council sponsored writing contests seeking books for children about various cultural groups. Some of those contest winners received publishers' contracts. It was hoped that the force of example combined with social forces would promote continued response and inclusion. To some extent, this was true. Some authors who entered the market at that time have sustained their careers. However, the entry of new authors is somewhat limited, though improved. When the acute interest of the society subsided with the quieting of civil rights protests, interest waned. The changing nature of publishing from smaller independent houses to large corporate entities also affected interest in social responsibility. (For information about the Council on Interracial Books, see an article by Beryle Banfield, "Commitment to Change: The Council on Interracial Books for Children and the World of Children's Books," *African Review* [Spring 1998].)

NEWBERY WINNERS CRITICIZED

Although production of children's materials about African Americans had increased, every book given an award was not equally welcomed by the literary and library communities. Subtle and blatant evidence of racism was discussed in library literature and elsewhere. What may have been well-meaning efforts were questioned. Criticisms appeared about past titles having received the award, such as 1923 medal winner *The Voyages of Doctor Dolittle*. Isabella Suhl asked the question in her article about this book: "How many more generations of black children must be insulted by them—how many more white children allowed to be infected with their message of white superiority?"[9]

The book *Sounder*, which received the Newbery Award in 1970, was challenged by Caucasian critics, joining African American voices of concern. About this book Albert V. Schwartz asked, "Does it accurately present the Black perspective?"[10] He is also quoted as saying, "Take the Newbery Award for example, which is often given not so much because the book is good but sometimes because it's popular. I think *Sounder* (Harper) won the award because of the black experience, not because the book was good."[11]

Highly controversial was the 1974 Newbery Award winner titled *The Slave Dancer*, one of the first winners centered around the slave trade. Sharon Bell Mathis, a teacher and author of the 1976 Newbery honor book, *The Hundred Penny Box*, wrote an article titled "*The Slave Dancer* Is an Insult to Black Children." She stated:

> Children's books have always reflected the society they flourished in. There was a time when people thought that books had to be very tiny because children were very small. We laugh about that

now, but that was very serious at the time, "little books for little people." There was another time when children had to read the most terrible, the most frightening literature to make them good, to make them courteous, to make them understand that God was important. Now we recognize the mistakes. I wonder years from now, what people will recognize as our mistakes.[12]

She was distressed about the images that would be planted in the minds of children, such as a crew member stating about the slaves, "They don't think much,"[13] and comparisons of slaves to captors such as, "Cawthorne [the captain] knew the black would recover—they can survive floggings that would kill a white man a hundred times over."[14]

Another article about the same book endorsed Ms. Mathis's response and called attention to more subtle matters, such as the boy who "danced the slaves" being designated as Creole. Although the dictionary definition of Creole allows that the word could apply to almost any person of mixed heritage, it was pointed out that in many parts of the African American community, Creole implied an African American with Louisiana heritage, sometimes with very light skin.[15]

Perhaps visibility and longevity are the central issues regarding the Newbery Award, which remains the most prestigious award for this genre. Books selected cannot be taken lightly. Although many children's titles might have short lives in print, books on the Newbery list remain in print for long periods. Some out-of-print titles return to print periodically. Trusting the literary judgments of the Newbery committee, these are the books to which teachers often give priority in literature assignments. Numerous online teachers' guides and lesson plans can be found for Newbery titles. Such issues as an author's fairness in presenting racial issues and accurate delineation of multicultural settings should be important award considerations. Since publishers seek books they hope will sell, literary critics determining an award such as the Newbery have the added responsibility of knowing the impact of this award and its lasting promise to each title selected.

In part, the Coretta Scott King Book Award was initiated to ameliorate the problems already discussed. Many librarians believed that giving an award demanding review of all materials for a given year by and about African Americans would help focus attention on Black authors and themes. Although the King Award does not have recognition factors equal to those of the Newbery, it brings attention to a greater number of books about persons of African descent and to those by African American authors. The Coretta Scott King Award has become respected in educational circles and is highly recommended for the broadest perspectives of Africans and African Americans in its selections. Numerous state and local libraries also provide lists that provide guidance.

GUIDELINES FOR THE NEWBERY AWARD

Many of the issues discussed above may seem extraneous to views of literature, but award criteria call for such things as "accuracy" and "clarity," which would directly apply to cultural omissions and to such things as the use of plantation dialect, which is hard to understand. The repetitive stereotypes of African Americans such as "huge" and "bug-eyed" apply to the delineation of characters. Stories that ignore the historical presence of African Americans have certainly not truthfully portrayed the setting. The issues and criteria are therefore congruous.

The complete text of the terms and criteria for the Newbery Award, which is available to all from the American Library Association (ALA), follows. (Italicized are areas to which considerations in this text could apply. These current terms were found at the ALA website—written in 1978 and revised in 1987. Earlier criteria may vary substantially.)

TERMS and CRITERIA
John Newbery Award

Terms

1. The Medal shall be awarded annually to the author of the most distinguished contribution to American literature for children published in English in the United States during the

preceding year. There are no limitations as to the character of the book considered except that it be original work. Honor Books may be named. These shall be books that are also distinguished.

2. The award is restricted to authors who are citizens or residents of the United States.

3. The committee in its deliberations is to consider only the books eligible for the award, as specified in the terms.

Definitions

1. "Contribution to American literature for children" indicates the text of a book. It also implies that the committee shall consider all forms of writing—fiction, non-fiction, and poetry. Reprints and compilations are not eligible.

2. A "contribution to American literature for children" shall be a book for which children are a potential audience. The book *displays respect for children's understandings, abilities, and appreciations.* Children are defined as persons of ages up to and including fourteen, and books for this entire age range are to be considered.

3. "Distinguished" is defined as:
   • marked by eminence and distinction; noted for significant achievement
   • marked by excellence in quality
   • marked by conspicuous excellence or eminence
   • individually distinct

4. "Author" may include co-authors. The author(s) may be awarded the medal posthumously.

5. In defining the term, "original work," the committee will consider books that are traditional in origin, if the book is the result of original research and the retelling and interpretation are the writer's own.

6. "American literature published in the United States" means that books originally published in other countries are not eligible.

7. "Published . . . in the preceding year" means that the book has a publication date in that year, was available for purchase in that year, and has a copyright date no later than that year. A book might have a copyright date prior to the year under consideration. If a book is published prior to its year of copyright as

stated in the book, it shall be considered in its year of copyright as stated in the book. The intent of the definition is that every book be eligible for consideration, but that no book be considered in more than one year.

8. "Resident" specifies that author has established and maintained residence in the United States as distinct from being a casual or occasional visitor.

9. The term, "only the books eligible for the Award," specifies that the committee is not to consider the entire body of work by an author or whether the author has previously won the award. The committee's decision is to be made following deliberation about books of the specified calendar year.

10. The term, "in English" means that the committee considers only books published in English. This requirement DOES NOT limit the use of words or phrases in another language where appropriate in context.

Criteria

1. In identifying "Distinguished Writing" in a book for children,
   a. Committee members need to consider the following:
      - Interpretation of the theme or concept
      - Presentation of information including accuracy, clarity, and organization
      - Development of a plot
      - Delineation of characters
      - Delineation of setting
      - Appropriateness of style

      Note: Because the literary qualities to be considered will vary depending on content, the committee need not expect to find excellence in each of the named elements. *The book should, however, have distinguished qualities in all the elements pertinent.*
   b. *Committee members must consider excellence of presentation for a child audience.*

2. Each book is to be considered as a contribution to literature. The committee is to make its decision primarily on the text. Other aspects of a book are to be considered only if they distract from the text. Such other aspects might include illustrations, overall design of the book, etc.

3. The book must be a self-contained entity, not dependent on other media (i.e., sound or film equipment) for its enjoyment. Note: The committee should keep in mind that the award is for literary quality and quality presentation for children. The award is not for didactic intent or for popularity.

Adopted by the ALSC [Association for Library Service to Children] Board, January 1978. Revised, Midwinter, 1987.

CONTINUING ISSUES AND CONCLUSIONS

The issues cited above definitely continue. In 1994 Lani Guinier wrote *The Tyranny of the Majority, Fundamental Fairness in Representative Democracy*. In the foreword Stephen Carter states: "The point rather is to recognize that we yet live in a nation in which every black nominee comes before the Senate and the public with a particular cross to bear: the need to dispel a set of assumptions about work ethic, rationality, and intelligence."[16]

What are the sources of such assumptions? They do not exist simply because people look different. In our world, separate cultural and racial communities remain isolated. Racial assumptions are created sometimes by outright racist teachings, by exclusions from the mainstream media, by the value judgments of even well-meaning parents, by exclusions from historical narratives, and by negative portrayals and exclusions in literature.

NOTES

1. W. E. Burghardt DuBois, *The Souls of Black Folk, Essays and Sketches* (Greenwich, Conn.: Fawcett Publications, Inc., 1961), 137.

2. See Theodore Taylor, *The Cay* (New York: Doubleday, 1974) in *Cultural Conformity in Books for Children, Further Readings in Racism*, edited by Donnarae MacCann and Gloria Woodard (Metuchen, NJ: Scarecrow Press, 1977), 93, 102, 163, 165.

3. Augusta Baker, "Guidelines for Black Books: An Open Letter to Juvenile Editors," in *The Black American in Books for Children*, edited

by Donnarae MacCann and Gloria Woodard (Metuchen, NJ: Scarecrow Press, 1972), 50–62.

4. Walter Mosley and others, eds., *Black Genius: African American Solutions to African American Problems* (New York: W. W. Norton & Co.,1999), 217.

5. John Hope Franklin, *From Slavery to Freedom: A History of Negro Americans, Fifth Ed.* (New York: Alfred A. Knopf, 1980), 33.

6. Franklin, *From Slavery to Freedom*, 35

7. Franklin, *From Slavery to Freedom*, 165

8. William Loren Katz, *Black Indians, A Hidden Heritage* (New York: Atheneum, 1986).

9. Isabella Suhl, "The 'Real' Dr. Doolittle," in *The Black American in Books for Children*, ed. MacCann and Woodard, 78–88. Originally published in *Interracial Books for Children* 1, nos. 1 & 2 (1969).

10. Albert V. Schwartz, "*Sounder*: A Black or White Tale?" in *The Black American in Books for Children*, ed. MacCann and Woodard, 89–93.

11. Jane Granstrom and Anita Silvey, "Call for Help: Exploring the Black Experience in Children's Books," in *Cultural Conformity in Books for Children*, ed. MacCann and Woodard, 99 (quotes Schwartz).

12. Sharon Bell Mathis, "*The Slave Dancer* Is an Insult to Children" in *Cultural Conformity in Books for Children*, ed. MacCann and Woodard, 146–148.

13. Mathis, "*The Slave Dancer* Is an Insult to Children," 146.

14. Mathis, "*The Slave Dancer* Is an Insult to Children," 147.

15. Binnie Tate, "Racism and Distortions Pervade *The Slave Dancer*," in *Cultural Conformity in Books for Children*, ed. MacCann and Woodard, 150.

16. Stephen Carter, "Foreword," in Lani Guinier, *The Tyranny of the Majority, Fundamental Fairness in Representative Democracy* (New York: Free Press Division/Macmillan, Inc., 1994), xviii.

General Analysis of Newbery Titles in Historical Context, 1922-2009

FOLLOWING THIS GENERAL ANALYSIS, individual titles are reviewed in detail. Books including African and African American images selected for Newbery honors *do* seem to reflect historical and social attitudes of the time of publication. Titles selected in the earliest years of the award present some of the most problematic images.

1922–1930

Although Lincoln's Emancipation Proclamation had been declared years earlier in 1863, Africans in America were still primarily in limbo. The proclamation stated, "All persons held as slaves within any state, or designated part of the State, the people whereof shall be in rebellion against the United States, shall be then, thenceforward, and forever free." During this period, African Americas still struggled against repression through "Jim Crow Laws" in the South, allowed by the Supreme Court, and through segregation in the North sometimes as severe.

This period marked the advent of the Harlem Renaissance, which produced African American writers who "helped to promote the idea of a distinct and authentic cultural community. This community had its own spokesmen who, in years following the First World War, protested all the social and economic wrongs."[1] In

New York City, and in other places, African Americans were beginning to have an influence not only in adult literature but also on
music and other cultural phenomena. In children's literature, and
in the Newbery Award, African Americans were largely ignored or
were presented in condescending terms. In *The Story of Mankind*,
award winner of 1922, Africa is largely ignored, though there is
brief mention of Haiti and slavery in America. *The Voyages of Doctor Dolittle*, selected in 1923 for the top award, has been revised to
remove some of the stereotypes. Views of Africans were primitive
with racist overtones. Much attention may have been paid to this
title because of its continuing popularity. This is one of those titles
that parents and grandparents remember as being fun to read and
wish to pass on to their descendants. The older editions are still
available in many reference collections and on the Internet. In the
1925 honor title *Nicholas: A Manhattan Christmas Story*, the only
African American character is "Uncle Rastus," who drives a horse
and cart; and in the medal winner *Shen of the Sea*, 1926, the term
"blackamoor" is found. Not commonly used in America, this term
was used in many places as a negative reference to anyone African.
The word is thought to have been a contraction of Black and Moor.
Smoky the Cowhorse, the 1927 winner, sounds like a simple horse
story, but the horse is mistreated by a dark mixed-race Mexican
referred to as "the breed." In *Clearing Weather*, which won honors
in 1929, one character looks back romantically at slavery in Louisiana.

1930–1939

By this time, African Americans had formed many political organizations, become active and prominent in unions, entered profes-
sions from which they had been formerly barred, and had become
active in national politics. Their influence was felt throughout the
country because many had moved west in search of jobs. As historian John Hope Franklin writes, "After 1932, Negro legislators in
California, Illinois, Indiana, Kansas, Kentucky, New Jersey, New
York, Ohio, Pennsylvania and West Virginia became common-

place."[2] Segregation and prejudices still reared their ugly heads. Disparities were even found in Roosevelt's relief efforts during the New Deal. But there were programs that allowed some African Americans to receive home loans and farm loans. Deficits in education remained a major problem in all parts of the country, but particularly in the South. At the same time, African American schools and universities were beginning to produce highly enlightened and capable graduates. In books selected by the Newbery committee, African Americans were still being presented as almost cartoon characters.

In 1930, an honor title, *Little Blacknose,* about a train engine, compares the color of a man to that of the engine. The award winner of 1930, *Hitty, Her First Hundred Years,* attempts some sensitivity, but also falls victim to the politics of its time in presenting African American characters. In *Spice and the Devil's Cave,* an honor book in 1931, slaves are presented as almost inhuman. It becomes clear that, in these early stages, the Newbery Award committee, authors, and publishers were unconcerned about positive portrayals of persons of African descent.

Once in a while a surprise was encountered, such as the book *Garram the Hunter,* honor award, 1931, in which the author positively portrays an African boy as a hero.

Many early books and many later completely ignored the presence of Africans and African Americans. When presented, reference was often to servile roles, minstrel performers, and Uncle Tom–like characters. One particularly offensive title was *Floating Island,* honor winner, 1931. In a doll house, one of the dolls is Dinah the cook, coal black, with a kerchief, who feels more comfortable being "queen of the monkeys." *The Railroad to Freedom: A Story of the Civil War,* honor book, 1933, is a fictionalized biography of Harriet Tubman and the Underground Railroad. "Niggerisms" and "darkeys" abound in the text. The 1934 title *Invincible Louisa* has much more positive portrayals, as does *The Winged Girl of Knossos,* honor award that same year. *Swords of Steel,* receiving honors that year, is more realistic than some in portraying friendship between a Caucasian boy and a freed slave. A biography of Davy Crockett shows peripheral views of slaves, hunting, dancing, and otherwise

providing music—a 1935 honor book. It is no surprise that the
honored biography of Audubon does not clarify the African heritage
of this prominent figure. Exposing such heritage would have been
problematic on all fronts during this time. The biography won honors in 1937. In *Hello the Boat!*, 1939 honor book, the only African
American characters are minstrel performers, and even in one of
the revered Laura Ingalls Wilder books, her father dresses up in
blackface.

1940–1949

Franklin writes of this period, "In the succeeding years the fight for
graduate education continued. The issue was clearly defined in a
decision of a Texas state court that a Negro who applied for admis-
sion to the University of Texas Law School either must be admitted
or a law school had to be established for him that was substantially
equal to the one in existence."[3] Separate but equal had become
the norm as the African American struggle for better education
proceeded on many fronts. African Americans were still forced by
unwritten and written laws to live in separate communities, forming an important subculture on the American scene. The riddle
remained—what definition of freedom applied to African culture
in America? The early '40s were also the years of World War II.
America faced the world with a black army and a white army. Some
workers were able to improve their economic status by moving into
the defense industries. African Americas fought valiantly in that
war, only to return facing the same inequalities.

Attitudes toward African Americans in Newbery titles still dealt
with the slave image, as was true of the honor book *Boy with A
Pack*, 1940. This book, however, concentrated on helping slaves to
freedom. An odd reference to science in defining the *place* of African Americans is made by Louis Agassiz in his biography selected
for honors in 1940. Minor references are made in several titles during this period, but in the 1944 winner *Johnny Tremain*, peripheral
African American characters take on more importance than in the
past. *Abraham Lincoln's World* places emphasis on important his-

torical characters living during Lincoln's times, but *none* are African American. In 1948, the first collection of African tales honored was *The Cow-Tail Switch*. In 1949, the first definitive history of African Americans, *Story of the Negro*, written by the prominent writer Arna Bontemps, was given honors.

1950–1959

The separate but equal doctrine had continued since *Plessy v. Ferguson* in 1896, but in 1954 the *Brown v. The Board of Education* decision stated, "Separate educational facilities are inherently unequal. Therefore, we hold that the plaintiffs and others similarly situated for whom the actions have been sought are, by reason of the segregation complained of, deprived of the equal protection of the laws guaranteed by the Fourteenth Amendment." Truman assaulted and outlawed segregation in the armed services. The Fair Housing Act led to violence in neighborhoods when African Americans moved in. Cicero, Illinois, 1951, was one of the more famous cases. The Montgomery, Alabama, boycott began in 1956. Southern members of Congress denounced desegregation. African Americans continued the fight for fair employment, better housing, and other essentials of survival. Even more violence was on the rise. Franklin writes, "Dismissals from jobs, denials of loans, and foreclosures of mortgages were some of the tactics used to decimate the ranks of 'aggressive Negroes.'"[4] It was in 1957 that Governor Orval Faubus of Arkansas came to attention for opposing the integration of a high school. Federal troops were called up by President Eisenhower to protect the children. This was the same year that Ghana became the first African nation to join the United Nations. In Congress, attempts were being made to pass various civil rights bills, but all failed.

Anger and fear led to violence against individuals and groups. African Americans were faced by complacency and indifference in some quarters and economic, social, and political resistance to civil rights in others. We can guess that these events had an effect on everything. After the Newbery Award was given to *Amos Fortune* in 1951, few selected titles had references to African Americans. In

Rifles for Watie, there are images of slaves during the Civil War; and in the 1959 winner, *The Witch of Blackbird Pond*, the protagonist speaks about having owned slaves.

1960–1969

The revolution for civil rights had begun among African Americans and had garnered the support of many white politicians and social groups. It was 1965 when the Watts Revolt occurred after marches, protests, and the rise of Martin Luther King, Jesse Jackson, Stokeley Carmichael, and many, many more. Though hesitant, John F. Kennedy's intervention in and adoption of civil rights causes only led to more marches and attacks on the many barriers to progress now recognized by the nation. In February, 1960, African American students attending the all-Black college of A&T in Greensboro, North Carolina, sat down at a lunch counter. They were refused service, but they continued to sit until the store closed. This began the "sit-ins." Whites joined African Americans in many peaceful protests. Major changes began in the South and throughout the nation. The status of African Americans became a major question of concern, while in African American communities various movements toward self-determination and pride in race were telegraphed. The march on Washington, where Martin Luther King gave his famous "I Have a Dream" speech, took place in August 1963. This was the largest demonstration in the history of the nation's capital. Violence was the reaction of whites to the expanding marches and political changes. A church bombing killed four African American children and President Kennedy was assassinated in 1963. Lyndon Johnson, who followed Kennedy into office, passed the most far-reaching legislation affecting the lives of Blacks, the Civil Rights Act of 1964. Despite the law, repression continued. The fight for freedom progressed while reaction brought the deaths of Martin Luther King, Medgar Evers, and Bobby Kennedy. African Americans chose to refer to themselves not as "Negro" but as "Black" or "Afro-American."

During this period more approaches to African Americans appeared in literature for children and Newbery selections reflecting the positive movement began to appear. In 1966, *I, Juan de Pareja* received the medal. This fine portrayal of a person of African descent did not spotlight an African American but one of Spanish derivation. *The Jazz Man*, an honor book of 1967, featured an African American boy and his family in New York City. *The Egypt Game* and *Jennifer, Hecate, Macbeth, William McKinley, and Me, Elizabeth*, honor books of 1968, were the first Newbery selections to take a stab at interracial friendships. Julius Lester's *To Be a Slave* presented true narratives of ex-slaves.

1970–1979

In the 1970s, the African American presence was more prominent on the national and world scenes. The Black Congressional Caucus was strong. Shirley Chisholm vied for the presidential nomination of the Democratic party, and the National Black Political Convention met in 1972. Jesse Jackson's Operation PUSH strove for excellence in Black leadership and in the control of their communities. But many of the changes for which the African American appetite had been whetted were slow to come. Better jobs, better living conditions, and police repression were still matters of concern. But Blacks were prominent at all levels of government and while in 1976 about 31 percent of all Blacks still remained in poverty, a few Blacks attained millionaire status. African Americans had accumulated substantial wealth as early as the 1800s, but during this period, millionaires increased as entrepreneurs, in entertainment, and in sports. Positive images on television shows such as *Julia* and others helped improve perceptions of African Americans. Alex Haley's *Roots* was a blockbuster presentation.

The '70s saw an increase in the number of African American authors for children. The Newbery Award acknowledged the works of Virginia Hamilton, awarding her an honor for *The Planet of Junior Brown* in 1972 and the Newbery Medal for *M. C. Higgins the Great* in 1975. Sharon Bell Mathis received an honor award in 1976 for her title *The Hundred Penny Box*. Mildred Taylor was awarded the Newbery medal in 1977 for *Roll of Thunder, Hear My Cry*, and the

1979 winning title, *The Westing Game*, had a prominent, strong, and positive female character. Outstanding African American illustrators also were prominent during this period.

1980–1989

African Americans continued to move up into important positions in local, state, and national government. Advancement was seen in almost every area, including education and the sciences. A Black Family Summit was held at Fisk University in May 1984. On television visibility of African Americans was evident not only in programming but also in the presence of anchors and reporters such as Ed Bradley and Bryant Gumbel. Major organizations including the National Urban League continued to work on ways to improve race relations. Focus was placed on such areas as early childhood education, developing a self-sustaining economic base, voter registration, and increasing the number of African Americans in higher education. Many felt that lack of progress at the core of African American problems was simply because of benign neglect.

In portrayals of African Americans in the Newbery Award only one title reached back to slavery. The award-winning title *A Gathering of Days: A New England Girl's Journal, 1830–1832* presents a protagonist who is involved in helping runaway slaves. Refreshingly, Virginia Hamilton continued to be rewarded for excellence, receiving an honor award for *Sweet Whispers, Brother Rush* in 1983 and honors again in 1989 for her *In the Beginning: Creation Stories from Around the World*. The 1983 medal winner has one Black character, a school friend of the main character. The African American friend appears again in *A Solitary Blue*, an independent sequel that won honors in 1984. A school friendship between a Black male and a troubled Caucasian boy is created in *The Moves Make the Man*, honor book of 1985. Walter Dean Myers's *Scorpions* emphasizes the strong friendship between an African American boy and a Puerto Rican one. Integrating characters was now on the move. Other titles receiving honors doing this period were *Commodore Perry In the Land of the Shogun*, 1986, which reintroduces minstrels, and

Lincoln: A Photobiography, the 1988 winner, which has information about slavery and the Civil War and shows seldom-seen pictures of Black infantrymen of the period.

1990–1999

This period is marked by a re-migration of many African Americans to the South for economic and social reasons. New themes regarding the problems of race arise, such as the premise that race is not a scientific category but one used to deny Africans and African Americans access to wealth. Emphasis is again placed on "self-determination" as ethnic communities in major cities continue to disintegrate. From the ruins of the cities comes the rise of the "hip-hop" generation, with major impact on youth of all cultures.

The '90s were the years of focus on apartheid and sanctions upon South Africa. The rise of Nelson Mandela from prisoner status to that of a major statesman awakened the attention of the world. He won the Nobel Peace Prize in 1993 and was president of South Africa from 1994 to 1999. Mandela remains one of the major heroes of this period.

In 1991, *Maniac Magee* was the Newbery winner. It features a Caucasian boy adopted by an African American family. *The True Confessions of Charlotte Doyle* has an African American character who helps save the young, female, Caucasian protagonist. *The Dark-Thirty: Southern Tales of the Supernatural*, a collection of tales from southern Black culture, won honors in 1993. *The Ear, the Eye, and the Arm*, honor book of 1995, is a fantasy with African motifs.

It is understandable that a long time passed before someone tackled the killing of four black children in the 1963 church bombing. This is a difficult event to write about in a book for children. The 1996 honor book, *The Watsons Go to Birmingham—1963* does this in a positive African American family story.

In 1996, *Yolanda's Genius*, about a smart, young African American female, won honors. *A Girl Named Disaster*, honored in 1997, is set in Africa with a female heroine. The 1999 winner of the Newbery was *Holes*, an extremely creative novel, with African American male characters having strong roles. Images of African Americans in the award by this time show *definite* improvement.

2000–2009

Every year since 1973, the National Urban League has published *The State of Black America.* In the 2007 executive summary, the focus is on "Portrait of the Black Male," with a foreword by Senator Barack Obama. The 2007 document stated, "This year's index puts the status of African Americans at 73.3 percent of whites, up slightly from 2006's 73 percent. In other words, blacks made minimal progress on the equality front in the past year. Just as in 2006, they performed best in the civil engagement category at 105 percent of whites, and worst in economics with 57 percent."[5] Focus on empowering the Black community with attention to African American males was a prevalent theme during this period while the themes of education, employment and income, and poverty continued. The U.S. Census Bureau in 2000 reported that the poverty rate for Black Americans was three times the rate for white Americans. At the same time, the U.S. Commerce Department reported in March 2001 that 800,000 businesses were owned by Black Americans.

This period and certainly the years 2008–2009 will be marked by the rise of Barack Obama to become the first African American president of the United States. His message of "change" galvanized youth, the African American community, and others. His strategically advanced campaign, his cross-cultural presence, and the overall message of hope may be the vanguard for years to come.

Beginning with the award-winning title *Bud, Not Buddy*, the African American presence in Newbery titles continued to improve. This story set during the Depression years focuses on family ties. In *Hope Was Here*, honor book 2001, the author moves beyond interracial friendships between youths to one between adults. *Carver: A Life in Poems* and *The Voice That Challenged a Nation* are historical biographies, while *An American Plague: The True and Terrifying Story of the Yellow Fever Epidemic of 1793* provides little-known information about the prominent role of Blacks during this time.

Lizzie Bright and the Buckminster Boy takes a step further with a strong friendship formed between a white male and a young, female descendant of African American slaves. *Show Way*, honor book of 2006, has striking images in story and pictures. Honor book *Elijah of Buxton*, 2008, documents the establishment of African American settlements in Canada by escaped slaves through the story of a young boy of African heritage born in such a town. The 2009 honor book *After Tupac and D Foster* remarkably attacks social problems of African Americans. The author of this book, a young, female African American, has made several outstanding contributions to this genre. *The Surrender Tree: Poems of Cuba's Struggle for Freedom*, which also won honors, is an outstanding poetic portrayal of slavery in Cuban history.

Language

In many of the Newbery Award titles portraying African Americans, plantation-like dialect is used. This is especially true of those about slavery. Some of the derogatory language that African Americans use among themselves is questionable, though the negatives imposed on people are often absorbed into their culture and communication. In a fictionalized story of Harriet Tubman, *The Railroad to Freedom: A Story of the Civil War*, the plantation dialect is dense and her references to children, such as "you low-down black chile," even said "tenderly," are at the least insensitive (8). As the images improve gradually, so does the language. By the '50s, dialect had been improved somewhat but was still present. Most of the modern colloquial language, sometimes used, seems acceptable. The necessity for the negative references found in a few newer titles is questioned in the detailed reviews.

Roles

The earliest Newbery awardees presented no images of free Blacks, educated Blacks, Blacks in schools, and so on. With the exception of the title *Garram the Hunter: A Boy of the Hill Tribes*, it was 1951 before any title with an African or African American protagonist won the award. This title was *Amos Fortune, Free Man*. Some feared that this book may have been a little *too* romanticized, not allowing young people to realize the tragedy of slavery or the general plight of African Americans during the time that Amos Fortune lived or at the time of publication. Arna Bontemps's book *Story of the Negro*, which received an honor award in 1949, presents accurate, though muted facts. No other winners featuring African American protagonists appear until 1966, when the winner was *I, Juan de Pareja*, still one of the better of the award-winning books featuring persons of African descent. This was followed by *Sounder* in 1970, which caused much consternation because none of the African Americans were given names, only the dog. The book was made into a film, which was very well done because characters became more personalized and the images were evident.

African American authors delved into improved roles for Black characters. In 1977, Mildred Taylor's *Roll of Thunder, Hear My Cry* presents as a character one of the first strong African American fathers and an intact family fighting to keep their land. Sharon Bell Mathis's poignant and beautiful story *The Hundred Penny Box*, about a boy relating to his aged great-great-aunt, presents roles not often found in books about African Americans. Virginia Hamilton's *M. C. Higgins the Great* won the Newbery in 1975 with an unusual theme, setting, and protagonist. Before her untimely death, this author contributed many titles to the materials about African and African American culture. The detailed reviews that follow later will show a significant improvement in African American roles from about 1975 forward.

EMPHASIS ON SLAVERY

From the beginning of this award, several winning books included some aspect of slavery. Some books simply discuss the issue or give mild focus to the slave while others present actual scenes with slavers. In 1922 *The Great Quest*, an honor book, features a ship sailing to Africa and the Gulf of Guinea, with slaving one of the issues. In the 1929 honor title *Clearing Weather*, slavery is discussed in almost positive terms through the character Michael, who owned slaves. In the 1931 honor book *Spice and the Devil's Cave*, it is a Moor slave who rescues and travels with the girl of interest. In a book about George Washington titled *Leader by Destiny*, his ownership of slaves is duly noted. The author tries valiantly to project an image of positive relationships between a boy and a slave in *Swords of Steel*, an honor book in 1934. In that same year two other honor books mention slavery, *The Winged Girl of Knossos* and *Glory of the Seas*. Continuing into 1944, the Newbery winner of that year, *Johnny Tremain*, has a protagonist who encounters slaves and African American servants in the Boston area, just prior to the Boston Tea Party. The 1958 Newbery winner, *Rifles for Watie*, is set during Civil War years, and the protagonist encounters African American slaves and servants. *The Bronze Bow*, Newbery winner 1962, is set in Rome, but a black slave is captured to serve rebel boys protesting Roman captivity. In other honor books, the subject of slavery is discussed by characters.

In some books, passages emphasize the help given to slaves by the protagonist or major characters in the story. *Boy with a Pack*, winning honors in 1940, gives emphasis to saving runaway slaves. In several cases the role of the Quakers in such escapes is prominent. The 1934 Newbery winner, *Invincible Louisa*, depicts the noted writer Louisa May Alcott's involvement in slave escapes.

In biographies of such people as Davy Crockett, honor award in 1935, and Audubon, honor award in 1937, African American workers and slaves are presented simply as a normal part of life. Both use "negro" workers in their adventures. Some are pictured as dancing and singing. The slave image of African Americans continues into the 1950s, when the winner *The Witch of Blackbird Pond* has a Caucasian protagonist from Barbados, who grew up owning slaves. Even one of the most outstanding characters of African descent presented in *I, Juan de Pareja* was a slave, before being freed by his mentor and owner. This book was the Newbery winner in 1966. The controversy surrounding the Newbery winner *The Slave Dancer* has already been discussed. In 1969, Julius Lester

produced *To Be a Slave*, the only book for children that documents
the real attitudes of slaves from historical documents. A 2009 honor
book aptly deals with slavery in Cuba.

DESCRIPTIONS AND AESTHETICS

From the detailed reviews, it will be found that the terms "darky,"
"nigger," "kinky headed," and other negative descriptors are used
not only in titles selected in early years but in later ones as well. In
the Newbery Winner *Amos Fortune*, other terms were added such
as "dusky." There is continual repetition and focus on Africans
having "white eyeballs." It should be obvious that in a dark face,
eyes will seem whiter, but the presentations suggest some kind of
defect in these "white rolling eyes." In many cases the African male
encountered is "huge" or gigantic," even in titles set in more modern times, such as *Blue Willow*, where the only African American
male is a "huge negro." Being black is almost never presented in a
positive way. In the 1935 winner, *Dobry*, a very negative story is
told about a *black* Arab. Arabs and Africans are sometimes made
fun of in otherwise likeable titles, such as *The Middle Moffat*, referring to Zulu chiefs. There are a few exceptions, such as *King of the
Wind*, in which the great horse's companion and friend is a young
mute Arab. As mentioned before, *Garram the Hunter*, 1931, was far
ahead of its time. Instead of being pejorative, the author speaks of
the boy's black skin as "silky." In *The Winged Girl of Knossos*, more
positive descriptors are used than in others. The descriptions of
African American women are problematic, with the most positive
referring to them as "handsome." The author of *I, Juan de Pareja*
sees that an African slave of lighter hue is beautiful. Much later,
in 1997, *A Girl Named Disaster* has an attractive, female, African
protagonist.

In the 1970s, positive descriptors began to appear in writings
by African American authors and a few others. In the 1979 winner,
The Westing Game, an African American woman is a judge, the first
in her locale, and she is described positively. In *Philip Hall Likes
Me, I Reckon Maybe*, the main character is pert and self-confident.

In her books, Virginia Hamilton makes the greatest strides toward making the reader see Africanness in a different way. All of her books are progressive in this way, but especially her honor title of 1983, *Sweet Whispers, Brother Rush*, in which she describes the skin of a dark African American "like somebody red color some chocolate . . . maybe chocolate left in the path of sundown" (125). The 2009 honor title *After Tupac and D Foster* does not shy away from descriptors, seeing Tupac as beautiful and with descriptive references to variations in skin color and nonnegative references to hair texture and style.

Some positive images appear through books that have outstanding pictures, including *The Hundred Penny Box* and *Show Way*.

THEMES

Of the titles whose primary focus is on Africans or African Americans, those titles dealing with slavery have already been cited. There are three titles that offer African and African American folktales: *The Cow-Tail Switch*, 1948; *The Dark-Thirty*, 1993; and *In the Beginning*, 1989; all honor books. Urban themes and African American families in these settings are the focus of *The Jazz Man*, 1967; *The Planet of Junior Brown*, 1972; *Scorpions*, 1989; *Sweet Whispers, Brother Rush*, 1983; *Somewhere in the Darkness*, 1993; and *After Tupac and D Foster*, 2009. Rural families are covered in *Sounder*; *Philip Hall Likes Me, I Reckon Maybe*; and *Roll of Thunder, Hear My Cry*. Hamilton's *M. C. Higgins the Great*, winner in 1975, is set in an Ohio mountain strip-mining area.

Biographies include *Audubon*, 1937; *Amos Fortune*, 1951; *I, Juan de Pareja*, 1966; *The Voice That Challenged a Nation*, 2005; and *Carver: A Life in Poems*, 2002, a poetic biography of George Washington Carver.

Biracial and interracial relationships appear in 1968 in the honor books *Jennifer, Hecate, Macbeth, William McKinley, and Me, Elizabeth* and *The Egypt Game*; these two titles were for younger readers. In the much more complex novel *The Moves Make the Man*, 1985, an African American boy befriends a troubled Caucasian boy. *Maniac Magee*, 1991, has a Caucasian boy being nurtured by an African American family. In *Holes*, 1999, boys of several cultures are characters in a juvenile detention center. *Lizzie Bright and the Buckminster Boy* has a Caucasian boy becoming very close to Lizzie, a young descendent of slaves. *Hope Was Here* moves forward even further, presenting positive friendships between Caucasian and African American adults.

After reading all of the books, it seemed important that currently writers are including African Americans as prominent peripheral characters with equal prowess as the Caucasian characters. Sporadically derogatory terms such as "darky" and "nigger" still appear. In some cases, authors rightfully present these as terms used by the ignorant or racist characters of a story, but in others, these are the accepted terms used by more sympathetic characters.

In some books, characters of African descent are allowed to establish serious friendships and other relationships with Caucasians, though sometimes in the face of community resentment. The use of dialect seems to have been abandoned for more emphasis on the *rhythm* of language differences.

Physical descriptions are mostly lacking in these books. In fairness, they are missing in many children's books, which may be the author's or editor's method of allowing all children to relate to characters. Those authors who have made significant attempts to provide descriptors are noted in the reviews that follow.

Materials given award consideration still focus on problems that have historically faced the African American community, such as civil rights issues, overcoming slavery, and the effects of racism. Even a collection of folktales that won honors had some of this focus. A few titles are set on the African continent. Caucasian characterizations, comparatively, focus on broader issues such as adolescent love, handling the death of a friend or a family member, fantasies, community, and adventure.

For books set in this country, one critical question still remains: How can an author provide a sense of place and completely ignore the presence of African Americans? For example, one selected book documents a family traveling across country. You would think the characters would have seen African Americans, passed through their communities, or bumped into them in the grocery store. Instead, some authors are content to focus entirely on the central character and rather insular surroundings. People of African descent have had a historical presence in other parts of the world. This fact, as well, is often ignored in the literature. Editors may prefer less description of settings and surroundings for younger audiences, but one of the criteria for the Newbery is "delineation of setting" (guidelines for the Newbery Award are listed above).

As the country has progressed, so have portrayals of Africans and African Americans in children's books and in selections for the Newbery Award. This is particularly true in the honor book selections. Evidence reflects greater cultural recognition. In a world exposed to global views and criticisms of democracy, Caucasian images can't be the only images projected. The Western European focus, however, still remains most prominent as children learn what and whom the nation and the world values. Communication, negotiation, and all levels of exchanges between various cultures of the world are foreseen in the future. Appreciation of cultures should be demanded in writings for children, for it is they who will inherit the mission for peace in the world.

NOTES

1. John Hope Franklin, *From Slavery to Freedom: A History of Negro Americans, Fifth Ed.* (New York: Alfred A. Knopf, 1980), 363.
2. Franklin, *From Slavery to Freedom*, 389.
3. Franklin, *From Slavery to Freedom*, 408.
4. Franklin, *From Slavery to Freedom*, 459.
5. National Urban League, *2007 State of Black America, Portrait of the Black Male, Executive Summary* (New York: National Urban League, 2007), 3. www.nul.org.
For a related bibliography, go to www.lib.usm.edu/~degrum/html/collectionhl/ch-afroamericanbib.shtm.

Reviews: Newbery Titles with African or African American Images

FOLLOWING ARE REVIEWS OF BOOKS that portray persons of African descent as the main focus or as secondary characters and that have received the Newbery Award or were honor books from 1922 to 2009. *All books with the slightest reference to Africans, African Americans, or slavery in America are listed.* In the case of nonfiction, books may present these characterizations in a historical or informational context. Three plusses (+++) suggests that this title is selected as one of the better or best presentations of images in the focal categories. (M) before some titles means the references to Africans or African Americans were very slight and therefore may seem of marginal importance to some.

1922

Newbery Award

***The Story of Mankind* by Hendrik Willem van Loon. Liveright.**

In a personalized style, van Loon narrates his version of man's history. His story of man is sometimes captivating but is primarily limited to Western developments. Excluding China, much of Africa, and other entities, he excused it by claiming to concentrate on those places that were of significance in changing the world.

At the beginning of the chapter titled "The American Revolution," he mentions that trading companies continued "the fight for more territory in Asia, Africa and America" (323). There is a paragraph dedicated to the French in Haiti: "Here in the year 1791 the French Convention, in a sudden outburst of love and human brotherhood, had bestowed upon their black brethren all the privileges hitherto enjoyed by their white master." The pact was rescinded, he notes, followed by years of warfare between Leclerc and Toussaint L'Ouverture, "the negro chieftain." More details are added about Haiti gaining independence (388). (The Haitian revolution alone could have filled volumes.)

Under the theme "emancipation," he discusses slavery in America, beginning with the introduction of slavery by the Spaniards and the attempts to use Indians as slaves, and van Loon poses a common stereotype that "the negroes were strong and could stand rough treatment" (422). Briefly, the rise of the abolitionist movements and the abolishment of slavery in England and France and by the Dutch are mentioned with the caveat, "The southerners, however, claimed that they could not grow their cotton without slave-labour" (423). At least he doesn't say that slaves were "needed" as is commonly suggested. Lincoln and the Emancipation Proclamation are given credence.

Honor Award

The Great Quest: A Romance of 1826 by Charles Boardman Hawes. Little, Brown (out of print).

Living in Topham, Massachusetts, Josiah Woods and his wealthy Uncle Seth are captivated by Cornelius, a smooth talker. He convinces Uncle Seth to fund the purchase of a brig for travel to Cuba and the coast of Africa. Cornelius's intentions are not noble and trouble later ensues.

On ship, Cornelius has established allies, and when trouble is faced in New Guinea, some follow him, leaving Uncle Seth distressed. The events in Guinea are a little complicated, but simply put, Cornelius wants to steal jewels hidden in a sacred hut. They enter the hut and are surrounded by angry natives. As the siege progresses and all seem doomed, Uncle Seth goes crazy and is killed. Some of the invaders escape, including Josiah and Cornelius. Meantime, Faith, the daughter of a missionary killed in the uprising, has joined the marauding group. There are more encounters on the brig as one called Neil wants the ship now to become a slaver. The ship is wrecked off the coast of South America and Neil drowns. Josiah, who has fallen in love with Faith, returns to Topham, expecting to face poverty. But upon his return Josiah learns that Uncle Seth had reserved a substantial sum, which he now inherits.

Regarding African or African American images, the native people protecting their land and property are referred to as "savage" Guineans. Although not frequent, there are negative terms used, none of which are surprising for the times: "'You will have half the niggers in Africa upon us'" (208); "'the despised Africa'" (209); and "'the black devils are hard upon us'" (214).

Concerning one among the ship's crew, it is said, "Ohara's long sojourn on the continent, which made him a 'black man' in the sense that he had come to believe, or at least more than half believe in the silly superstitions of the natives, had served him better by giving him an amazing knowledge of the country" (215). It's not clear if this was meant to be a positive statement or just a suggested way to survive.

The most indicting personal ethnic views are of the "big black" who was Faith's companion. When Josiah first encounters him and the girl, he speaks of his "black, grotesque face with *rolling eyes*" and of having unconsciously snatched his hand away from his touch, "lest it be bitten"(180). During the description of escape from the island, readers are presented with the much repeated characterization of the powerful African male. There are references to his "might" in an elongated scene and "the negro again fairly lifted us by his great strength" (303). There are far too many negative references to quote made by the crew and the main character. Views of Africans are seen at stops in Cuba as well as New Guinea. In the end, Faith's trusty companion travels home with them and becomes a loyal servant.

The Old Tobacco Shop: A True Account of What Befell a Little Boy in Search of Adventure by William Bowen. Macmillan (out of print).

During Freddie's fanciful wanderings, he enters the Gate of Wanderers after traveling to the City of Towers, an ecumenical setting described as having many booths and "the people in them were apparently of all nations of the earth, there were brown men and yellow men and black men, as well as white; men with slant eyes, round eyes, with flat noses with beak-noses, with wooly hair, with straight hair; there were turbans, and fezzes and hoods" (179).

At another booth, "behind the counter stood a lad of about twenty, very dark skin with snapping black eyes and shiny white teeth" (181). Though brief, such noncondescending images are rare in the early award-winning titles.

1923

Newbery Award

The Voyages of Doctor Dolittle by Hugh Lofting. Stokes.

In the Dolittle titles, a series of stories follows the exploits of Dr. Dolittle, who is able to speak to animals.

This book, which has since been released in a new edition, may be one of the most controversial among the award winners. In the foreword to the new edition of 2001, Patricia and Frederick Mc-Kissack write, "Lofting wrote at a time when women couldn't vote, African Americans were denied their most basic human rights, children had few rights, and European colonization of Africa and Asia was at its peak." They continue, saying that the original text reflects the times and "contain[s] material that is offensive and demeaning to people of color." The pair conclude that the book and its predecessor, *The Story of Doctor Dolittle*, reintroduced in 1997, are "marred by racially insensitive language and artwork." Stating their strong objection to censorship, the two add, "no book should undermine a child's self esteem" (ix–xii).

1925

Honor Award

(M) *The Dream Coach* by Anne Parrish. Macmillan (out of print).

A princess, a little Chinese emperor, and a French boy each take the dream coach on imaginative adventures. Some of the story-adventures are told in verse.

The only African image found was within the description of the princess's arrival: "Last came four gigantic blacks wearing loin cloths and enormous turbans of flamingo pink . . . carrying the tiny princess" (16). Notice the "*gigantic*" African appears.

Nicholas: A Manhattan Christmas Story by Anne Carroll Moore. Drawings by Jay Van Everan. G. P. Putnam's Sons. N.Y. (out of print).

A brownie hiding in the children's room of the library on Christmas Eve is joined by Nicholas, a boy about eight inches tall, who enters through the window. The two set out on a trip exploring and enjoying the sights of New York City. In the chapter, "Beyond the Bowery," enters "Rastus, one of the old uncles down from Harlem" (215). For several pages, the children travel with him through parts of the city. He is described as a "jolly black driver" and speaks with mild dialect ("sweet 'tater"). The short trip ends at the "play house" where good-byes are said to Rastus.

The portrayal of the old man is not necessarily negative. The use of "uncle" and "aunt" were the common salutations for African Americans at a time when few whites referred to Blacks as Mr. or Mrs.

1926

Newbery Award

(M) *Shen of the Sea* by Arthur Bowie Chrisman. Dutton.

It may be hard to believe that in the middle of this collection of award-winning Chinese folktales, there is found one page where rather gross characters are fighting—a one-legged hunchback and "a blackamoor who had no arms !!!!" (72). The term "blackamoor" would be considered by most as an offensive and archaic reference to anyone of African descent or with black skin.

Honor Award

(M) *The Voyagers: Being Legends and Romances of Atlantic Discovery* **by Padric Colum. Macmillan (out of print).**
    This series of tales about ocean travel includes mythological tales of Poseidon and Atlas. Other stories are of Columbus, Ponce de Leon, and more familiar explorers. Few images of persons of African descent appear except in the stories titled "Voyages of Saint Bendan," the Island of Smith is described and on the Fragrant Island, "the men were black too, and were seemingly begrimed by smoke . . . long armed and broad shouldered men, but they were stunted in size."

1927

Newbery Award

Smoky the Cowhorse **by Will James. Scribner (out of print).**
    Basically about a man's love for a horse, his loss of the horse, and the eventual recovery of the animal. The story presents a culprit, the thief, who is "a half-breed of mexican and other blood that's *darker*" (208). The mouse-colored horse was broken and trained by Clint, who searches for and eventually recovers the horse. After his encounter with the thief, who afterward is called "the breed," Smoky is unable to tolerate anyone who is *dark*. Can we be sure that a horse has the sensibilities to be forever negative toward persons because of their color? The stolen horse was grossly mistreated, but wouldn't this experience make the horse unable to trust any man? In an otherwise interesting and exciting story about the horse, these negatives are interjected.

1928

Honor Award

(M) *The Wonder Smith and His Son: A Tale from the Golden Childhood of the World* **by Ella Young. Longmans (out of print).**
Gubbaun Soar is the main character of this retelling of tales about the mythological Irish giant. Gubbaun laments having a daughter and not a son. He trades his daughter for a son whose only interest is music. Gubbaun doesn't know what to do with the son and wishes his daughter would return. In turn, the daughter is strong and productive. The foreword notes that in Gaelic-speaking Ireland and Scotland, tales of the "Gubbaun Soar" are well known.

An African presence might not be expected in Gaelic tales, but Gubbaun encounters the Count of Balor, described as the blackener of the earth, with one eye in the center of his forehead. "Eight slaves blacker than charcoal wood" appear (99).

1929

Honor Award

Clearing Weather **by Cornelia Meigs. Little, Brown (out of print).**
This story begins with ship making after the American Revolution. Thomas Drury, a once prosperous shipbuilder, is broke. His nineteen-year-old nephew, Nicholas, vows to save the family business from Darius Corland, Drury's creditor.

Nicholas hides a runaway Frenchman, Etienne Bardeau, and from this Frenchman, he learns information about Darius Corland. There are documents that implicate Corland in assisting the British during the revolution.

Nicholas and Michael Slade, his best friend, build a ship called *The Jocasta* and sail to the West Indies. Their adventures and perils are followed. The two decide that they can make more money by traveling east by way of Cape Horn. As they travel, they encounter storms and capture, but eventually they return home with a ship-load of goods.

In the meantime, Corland's exploits have been discovered. He has been forced to leave for England and the Drury business is saved. The townspeople who contributed to building the ship share in the profits.

Images of African Americans appear through stories told by both Michael and Etienne. Michael tells about living on a planta-tion in the South in a big white house with "rows of tiny cottages which were the slave quarters. . . . Negroes picking cotton in the hot sun, or sitting at the doors of their cabins in the evenings, singing all together in the warm darkness." He told about raccoon hunts, saying, "Then some agile black youth would go shinning up the trunk to shake down the snarling 'coon" (115).

Etienne tells the story of an encounter on a wharf in Charles-ton. The British by accident "chanced to hear me speak in my own tongue to a Negro longshoreman from New Orleans." A fight en-sued, and "when his men saw him fall they closed in on me, and my one-time friend, the black, being a fellow of no bold heart, made off across the docks, his voice uplifted in terror" (43). Others helped Etienne escape.

1930

Newbery Award

Hitty, Her First Hundred Years by Rachel Field. Mac-millan.

These are the chronicles of a doll that travels from one home to another and from one owner to another. Although not as negative as some, found in this title are numerous condescending references to African Americans, which are typical of the times. When owned by Clarissa Pryce, the doll is aware that the Pryces are Quakers, involved in protests against slavery, and she hears their reading of

Uncle Tom's Cabin to Clarissa (126). Sympathy for the plight of the characters is expressed. Hitty also learns of Abraham Lincoln and the Civil War (128).

For a long while, Hitty was owned by Mr. Farley, who "kept me packed in a box with his best camel's-hair brushes." When they arrive in New Orleans, they live in the French Quarter with two older sisters, Miss Annette and Miss Hortense, "and a Negro woman still older, who had been a slave in the family before the war" (156). Sometimes Farley took Hitty out on the balcony, where "there were so many black people always going by—women with bright calico round their heads, others balancing baskets on theirs as lightly as if they had nothing in them, old men and young calling their wares in soft, deep voices" (157).

Later, Hitty is stolen from an exposition by young Sally and travels south with the girl and family on a boat called the *Morning-Glory*. Here she encountered "fields of cotton and sugar cane where black people were at work." At one docking, Sally goes to an African American church, finding "they were all black and beaming . . . and some had tiny brown babies in their arms." The preacher gives a sermon in mild (complex for children) dialect: "'I is gwine to tell you one thing sure an' dat is if you breaks de eight' commandment dat says: "Thou shalt not steal," you is gwine to be berry sorry'" (170). Sally begins to feel guilt about having stolen Hitty. Subsequently, there is a detailed, intense religious service, baptism in a river, and fervor among the crowd described as "a perfect frenzy" (171). These passages seem to make fun of the people and their religious passion.

When guiltily discarded by Sally, Hitty is found by "Car'line," an African American child, who is said to have resembled Topsy in *Uncle Tom's Cabin*. Speaking of the doll, "dat ma chile," Car'line says (174). About living with Car'line and family, Hitty comments, "I liked to hear them sing, for their voices were softer and sweeter than those of any children I ever met before" (175). More detailed discussion of the music, including banjos and spirituals, follows. For a Christmas party, "Car'line herself was resplendent in *turkey red*, her hair in tight little braids" (176).

There is also one questionable remark when Hitty is being sold at auction: "I am sure no slave on the block was ever more surprised at her own value than I" (201).

In this title, one can almost feel the author's struggle to present a sympathetic image of African Americans that would be acceptable during those times. She was probably limited also by her own knowledge.

Honor Award

Little Blacknose: The Story of a Pioneer by Hildegarde Swift. Harcourt (out of print).

Little Blacknose represents the De Witt Clinton Engine, the first locomotive for New York Central. It makes the trip from Grand Central Station to upstate New York. According to the story, the train was part of an exhibit at the Chicago World Fair and was a historical exhibit on one end of Grand Central Station.

The humanized train says, "'A tall black man strode through the crowd holding what looked like long strips of newspaper.'" The train thinks, "'This man is the right color. I wonder if he was born in the foundry. I wonder why all can't be that nicer shade like mine.'" It is obvious the man is a ticket agent or conductor; porters would not be carrying tickets. Going on, the man is shown waving the tickets and announcing, "'Dese tickets am done contracted foh.'" This is certainly unnecessary dialect for one in this position and more follows: "'Is you-all Mr. Beers, and is dis chile Thomas Beers? Yas, sah? Den dese is yo tickets foh shure, suh!'"

1931

Honor Award

Floating Island by Anne Parrish. Harper (out of print).

Racial stereotypes are rampant in this title designed with all of the elements necessary to charm the young. The characters are those who live in a dollhouse including the cook: "Dinah the cook was jointed but her head wouldn't turn. She was made of wood, painted black, with big white eyes and a red mouth as round as a berry." Her dress and turban are described, all bright colors. The story continues as the dollhouse is lost at sea and ends up on an island.

There are too many negative references to record here. But one of importance is Dinah's wish to have "yellow hair like Mrs. Doll's." Even more offensive is the finding of monkeys on the island and Dinah's refusal to leave them because she considers them more like family. She does not leave when the rest of the doll family is rescued. Reading this story and viewing the offensive illustrations indicate that the selection committee that gave this book an award must have had no racial sensitivity. (It is also very enlightening that Internet reviews of this book reveal that there are adults who consider this one of their early childhood favorites and wish to share the story with their young relatives.)

+++*Garram the Hunter: A Boy of the Hill Tribes* by Herbert Best. Doubleday (out of print).

Garram, son of the chief, is the most outstanding hunter in his tribe. He loves to hunt but has great respect for the animals and the rest of nature. His nemesis is Menud, a jealous competitor. Menud tries to use trickery and deceit to defame Garram.

Garram eventually travels with his dog, Kon, to other parts of his land, where he discovers an Arab city. After a few mishaps in the market, he is taken to the emir. The emir establishes a near father-son relationship with the boy and even disguises himself so that the two of them can go hunting together. It is Garram who helps to unravel a plot against the emir. The emir vows to be ever grateful to Garram. Later, it is revealed to the boy that an army of the Fulani of the East plan to cross through Garram's homeland to attack the emir. Garram realizes that he must return home.

Garram is presented as a true hero, with no condescension. The author does not shy away from attempts at aesthetic descriptions. Early in the story he describes perspiration running down "the silken black skin of the young hunter," "his clean cut build," and his "long thin muscles" (4). This is an outstanding adventure and hunting story, unusual for the times. The author's appreciation for African culture is evident.

Meggy MacIntosh by Elizabeth Janet Gray. Doubleday (out of print).

Of Scottish heritage, Meggy MacIntosh runs away and travels to America in search of her heroine, Flora MacDonald. She joins others of her clansmen in North Carolina. Early in the story she listens to stories told by Willie, who left America when he was six, but it was noted that "Negroes wandered in and out of his tales." He is quoted, "'Negroes were everywhere. Everybody had a nigger servant just for himself'" (72). Upon arrival in Wilmington, Meggy has her first experience with people of African descent. They serve the food: "The black servants kept passing more. In spite of herself, Meggy drew back a little when the Negroes passed. . . . They were so black and strange: she did not want them to touch her" (92–93). More descriptors occur: "followed by a string of small black kinky heads" (157) and "a little darky with a basket" (185) are examples.

As far as language goes, the story provides few occasions when African Americans speak. In one case, a servant is spoken *about* and her dialect imitated, "'I tell Daphne what to do . . . and she says, 'Yassum, ah sho' will,' with the greatest earnestness, but I know 'tis all gone out of her kinky head before she leaves the room!'" (235). Mrs. Malcolm is speaking. It is the Scottish dialect that is even more disconcerting than some attempts at presenting African American dialect.

Spice and the Devil's Cave by Agnes Hewes. Knopf (out of print).

Historical information is provided in this novel about the rivalry between Arab, Venetian, and Portuguese traders all seeking to cash in on the availability of treasured spices in Asia. There is mention of Diaz, da Gama, and Magellan, all living in Lisbon at the time and all seeking their fortunes through sources for spices.

Most of the drama and interesting parts of the story surround a beautiful and mysterious Arab girl called Nejmi. When discovered,

Ferdinand wonders about the girl's nationality and whether she is a slave, "'but slaves are black as ebony . . . and this girl has skin—well—like ivory, with sunlight striking across it.' . . . 'We can very soon find out at the docks whether any slave ship has put in here'" (12). As it turns out, the girl *had* been sold as a slave. Scander, one of the crew who knew about the girl, speaks of seeing her when returning to his ship, "'the only white thing among those black cattle with their big, white teeth and lips that thick!'" indicating by holding his fingers apart (92). Scander continues by saying that he did everything he could to trace Nejmi, figuring that he could recognize her by her fair skin. In Alexandria he discovers her again: "'I was just in time to see a big handsome chap—a moor he was—in seaman's dress, leading her away'" (93).

Scander is also speaking when the discovery of natives processing spices is discussed, "'sweaty half naked natives with their brown arms and hands . . . *their black eyes that sort of slipped around in their heads*'" (82). This is followed by a gruesome scene where the natives are slaughtered. There are many much too obvious racial epithets.

1932

Honor Award

(M) *Jane's Island* by Marjorie Allee. Houghton.

A young college student, Ellen, is the nanny for the daughter of a researcher on the island. Ellen and her younger charge spend many moments fishing, picnicking, and so forth, giving the reader a view of the island's ambiance. Other characters include Dr. Thomas and a German, Doctor VonBerger, doing scientific marine experiments in the 1920s. The seaside village is called Woods Hole.

The author presents only one African American image, the chauffeur, who appears at a big party to bring regrets and flowers from his employer: "'Mrs. Berry say she sho' was sorry she indisposed today and could not come to the party: but she send this li'l remembrance from her gyarden'" (85).

+++*Out of the Flame* by Eloise Lownsbery. Longmans (out of print).

No images of Africans are found in this story about the Renaissance in France. The adventures are those of Henri and Pierre. Emphasis is placed on the importance and the beauty of art and writing. The story is noted here for one laudable brief passage, when Pierre remembers being taught, "to you my son, all men, everywhere, no matter the race or color or creed will be brothers and friends" (280).

1933

Honor Award

The Railroad to Freedom: A Story of the Civil War by Hildegarde Swift. Illus. by James Daughtery. Harcourt Brace (out of print).

At the beginning of the book, the author's long interest in the life of Harriet Tubman is noted. There is also a prologue of various voices about slavery. First voice: "Slavery is wrong." Second voice: "Slavery is right. . . . It has produced the finest flower of civilization . . . the leisure of the luxurious South." It ends with many voices saying that war is the only solution.

As the story of Harriet Tubman is told, the dialect is sometimes hard to read and one might question the words placed into the mouth of Harriet and others. In one case Harriet is quoted, "'You low-down black chile,' she said tenderly. 'You is shure perverse!'" (8).

Descriptions of African American children are the typical ones, such as "four little kinky-headed children were playing" (14).

From the beginning, Harriet has plans to one day run away. The white-black relationships are shown as complicated. Blacks are prohibited from singing "Go Down Moses." Harriet begins the song and is joined by others. The half-white overseer rushes in and grabs Harriet, promising punishment, but it is the *master* who enters and saves her.

The same old arguments from whites about the reason for slavery are interjected: "Only the African could endure the heat of the cotton fields. . . . Only the African could face the toil of bondage and remain light-hearted and unembittered!" (23–24). The terms "niggah" and "nigger" are used repeatedly, by blacks and whites. "Darkies" is also commonly used. There is a disclaimer at the end of the book indicating that such terms are used for purposes of realism.

Harriet's eventual escape is cited and her many returns to free others. "Harriet became a myth, a legend, a figure of romance" (206).

The sources for the author's factual information are noted and a bibliography appended. This fictional biography of an African American heroine is terribly flawed.

1934

Newbery Award

+++*Invincible Louisa: The Story of the Author of* Little Women by Cornelia Meigs. Little, Brown.

An interesting and deserving biography is presented. Early in the story of Louisa May Alcott's life she is saved by a Negro boy: "A young Negro boy had seen the mischance and had sped to the rescue, quicker than any other. . . . He plunged in, brought Louisa safe to shore." He then apparently slipped away in the commotion. This incident is said to have always been remembered by Louisa, reminding her of the kindliness of the race. One day, she hears a sound from the kitchen's brick oven. "She opened the door and peeped in. A face looked out at her, a black face, gaunt, and as wild and desperate as a hunted animal's." After running to her mother, she was told about runaway slaves and the help being given to assist them in finding freedom in Canada (48–49). Notes about these incidents were found in Louisa's own record of her life. The story continues with detailed discussions about slavery and the politics of the time, other people in the community helping fugitives (90–91), and even the marriage of two runaways who wished to be married as others were.

Readers learn about some of the complexities of Louisa's life and family, including relationships with many of the Bostonian leaders of the time. Passages about Louisa's work as a nurse during the Civil War are included. Her writing is described as are her later fame and popularity.

Honor Award

Glory of the Seas by Agnes Hewes. Knopf.

The magnificent role of ships in early America is reviewed but also recognized is the negative role of many shipowners and builders in the slave trade.

News of the *Flying Cloud* has appeared in the paper while John and his Uncle Asa Wentworth, a judge, wonder how they should respond to the new Fugitive Slave Act. Uncle Asa is an abolitionist.

Uncle Asa has been involved in helping escaped slaves and John inadvertently becomes involved himself. The complications of confronting the law are clear as the story evolves. Issues are delineated through conversations. In a discussion with John, Taylor says John would be surprised "at the number of Yankee vessels that slip over to the Guinea coast for a load of black men and then smuggle 'em into the South" (90). John and the judge discuss fees for the capture of fugitive slaves: "I've heard that they are as high as five hundred dollars per slave" (114).

Descriptors are few. John, sitting on the wharf, talks to a negro: "Negroes amused him with their easy drawl and their good natured ways." Later he discovers the same man, an escapee, "at his very heels a big barefooted negro was panting out inaudible words from dry lips. Under the black skin the face was gray and the whites of the eyes bulged with terror."

The dialect is mild: "Sat'dy night, boss! White folks' baff night ain't it." "Niggerisms" are few and spoken by supporters of slavery, and in one case a drunk who exposes John's rescue by bumping into the escaped slave says, "Hey Blackface . . . I'll teach you to knock white folks down! . . . Stop, nigger!!!"

In this book, negative inferences *do* seem to be attempts to provide historical accuracy. It is an example, though, of how hard it was for many authors to provide a story where the African slave was brave. In this case, the slave, because of his fear, is recaptured, to John's disgust.

+++*Swords of Steel: The Story of a Gettysburg Boy* by Elsie Singmaster. Illus. by David Hendrickson. Houghton, Mifflin (out of print).

Although John hears conversations portending trouble, his life is good. He spends time with his beloved friend Nicholas, a free black, who lives nearby. The boy loves Nicholas and tries to imitate the way he talks. Nicholas takes care of horses and John intends one day to have a horse of his own. Slowly but surely as the story continues the family becomes embroiled in the politics of the day including issues of slavery, Lincoln's election, and eventually the rights and wrongs of the Civil War.

John is devastated when marauding gangs capture Nicholas to sell him to Southern slavers. He cries and seeks help, but Nicholas is not found nor discovered until much later in the story when the Civil War has already started and people have chosen gray or blue. Nicholas, only a shadow of his former self, is with the Southern armies serving as a caretaker and general slave to the group. He has only a brief time to renew his acquaintance with John but can't let their friendship be known.

When the war ends, John seeks news of Nicholas, only to find that he is dead. The book starts when John has just turned ten, but at the end he has become a man, by way of his experiences of six years.

After a somewhat jumbled beginning, where it is not easy to delineate all the characters, this is one of the better stories about the conflicts faced by families forced into war and the blood and slaughter during the Civil War. John's affection for Nicholas is not at all condescending, though some other references to relationships between free blacks and whites may seem so.

Dialect used is not overwhelming: "When John thought of Nicholas, he talked as Nicholas talked. 'Ise goin' to see him,' he said" (2). Nicholas speaks, "'Dis yeah Hotspur suah is libely. Whoa dah, hoss!'" It is obviously an example of how troublesome is the effort to translate dialects into print.

Very few physical descriptors are used except "coal-black" and "two little children and a black woman who wore a brilliant red turban" (46).

+++*Winged Girl of Knossos* by Erick Berry, pseud. (Allena Best). Illus. by the author. Appleton-Century (out of print).

Presented is an unusual story of Ancient Crete. Before the plot begins, it is noted that the palace of Knossos welcomed traders from Egypt, Sicily, Africa, and more.

Inas, who is on a boat fishing for sponges, seems to be recognized as being of darker heritage through descriptions of her brown face and tangle of black hair.

Tribal wars and conflicts are chronicled, and the relationship between Inas and Kadmos is an issue of growing importance. Regarding the current conflicts, Inas speaks to Kadmos regarding her father: "He is angry too, about the hiring of mercenaries from the south, black men, to enlarge the army" (29).

Further indications of Africa's proximity and influence are indicated as we meet Teeta, Inas's maidservant, described as having "dark skin, full mouth and kinky hair" (46). Inas loves Teeta, and her skills are valued. There is also mention of the power of cities of North Africa and Crete's jealousy of their progress. When Greek slaves try to escape from the palace, "two tall black soldiers from the land to the south" guarded the entrance (122).

Another major African presence is Mufu, a servant boy. Following is one description when Mufu appeared in Inas's doorway "his black face beaming and his kinky locks standing straightout, as though newly washed. Usually they lay quite flat to his head with oil and much patting." The description in this case is important because a ring which has been lost or stolen is hidden in his hair. None of these descriptors seems to have been meant to be condescending.

In an afterword, the author states that the entire story admittedly is created from the limited knowledge available about the area because of destruction from fire: "No one to this day knows who were the mysterious raiders that, in the absence of the Fleet, burned Knossos and the other great towns of Crete" (248). Archaeologists have uncovered some new information, but apparently there is still much to learn.

1935

Newbery Award

***Dobry* by Monica Shannon. Viking (out of print).**
The story is of a young Bulgarian peasant who has a talent for drawing and sculpting. His mother worries about his time spent doing artwork and not learning about and participating in the work of the farm that is his heritage. Dobry's grandfather is known as the farm community's resident storyteller. His stories are interspersed throughout the novel, though the focus is on the boy's desire to become an artist. Eventually, Grandfather is able to convince his mother that Dobry should go to art school.

It seems unusual to find any images of Africans or African Americans in a story focused on the mores, celebrations, dress, housing, and so on of peasant Bulgarians. But on one occasion, Grandfather tells the story of Hadutzi-Dare: "In those days, away behind now, the Black Arab on a horse" is a conquering Arab who ruthlessly attacks peasant communities. Residents are terrorized. "If a peasant ventures out of his house, taking a starving cow to pasture or a pig to market, the Black Arab steals the animal and rides the peasant down" (60). It is Hadutzi-Dare who conquers the Black Arab. The story goes on for about three pages, emphasizing the evilness and power of the Black Arab until Hadutzi-Dare "clubs the Arab down . . . [and] drops the Black Arab into one of the wells" (65). The story he tells is a fantasy, but the images are powerful.

Honor Award

Davy Crockett **by Constance Rourke. Harcourt (out of print).**
The author presents a fictionalized biography of the legendary
Davy Crockett, about whom many tall tales have been written.
Here, Crockett is presented as a real person who marries Polly Fin-
ley after being jilted by an earlier love. He is pictured as an adven-
turer, woodsman, and guide to the wilderness for other legendary
figures. Crockett is also credited with having fought in most of the
major battles of his time, including at the Alamo. He is shown to
be a naturalist and an excellent marksman. Polly is left behind to
care for house and family during his exploits. In his many absences,
Crockett takes Polly's loyalty for granted.

There are several encounters with African Americans during
Crockett's adventures. "Negro slaves made the music at the frolic,
thrumming a banjo or playing an old fiddle, shaking the bones.
. . . Some of them sat in the corner of the cabin at the reaping party,
singing fiddle tunes" (27). In another reference, "Two Negroes had
come in to light the bear oil lamps and were humming a sturdy little
tune. Crockett gave a turkey call. . . . The pair of Negroes answered,
gobbling, and began bending and strutting, leaning down to pick up
something from the ground as a turkey picks up corn." There are
other references to "the darkeys" and their singing and dancing and
to those who accompanied Crockett and friends on hunting trips and
escapades (46–47). For the most part, the encounters with African
Americans would be almost familial, had the author used only the
term "Negro" rather than "darky," even though both may be accurate
for the time. It is objectionable when authors continue to place emphasis on stereotypical African Americans' singing and dancing.

1936

Newbery Award

(M) *Caddie Woodlawn* **by Carol Ryrie Brink. Macmillan.**
Caddie Woodlawn is one of seven children who move with the
family from Boston to the Wisconsin prairie. The story follows one
year in the life, adventures, and troubles of Caddie and family.

Since Caddie's sister, the youngest daughter of the family, has died from frailty, father encourages Caddie to be a "tomboy" so that she will become strong. Caddie does, indeed. She plays with and follows her brothers in many escapades, including swimming across a river to visit Indian friends.

There are no real images of African Americans in the story, but there is a brief discussion of the Civil War. Although the author states, "the Civil War seemed remote to the children of western Wisconsin," some had gone to fight in the war, and Caddie's father had paid a man to fight in his place. During the visit by an itinerant minister from Boston, Father tells the minister as Caddie listens in her bedroom, "'If it weren't for my wife and children . . . Englishman and peace lover though I am, I should be out there fighting for abolition.'" The minister responds that English aristocrats see nothing wrong with slavery. Caddie's father answers, "'I am proud to say that I do not see things from the aristocratic point of view'" (25).

1937

Newbery Award

(M) *Roller Skates* by Ruth Sawyer. Viking.

While her parents are in Italy, Lucinda is left in the care of Miss Peters, who allows her to be mostly carefree. In the 1890s, Lucinda explores New York City. She is independent and feisty and travels mostly on her roller skates. Lucinda makes friends with the junkman, the patrolman, and a cab driver named Mr. Gilligan. Some intrigue develops, including a murder and the death of a child.

It is interesting that in New York City, none of the characters whom Cindy meets is African American. The only one who appears in this story is "Black Sarah," the cook.

Honor Award

***Audubon* by Constance Rourke. Harcourt (out of print).**

Introductory and appended notes give details about Audubon's heritage, presenting some of the questions but few answers as to whether Audubon was actually of African American heritage. From some other sources and references, the information seems to be conclusive regarding his African ancestry, but in this biography the question is left open. The author acknowledges that he was adopted by Captain Audubon and that the "question of his birth played a considerable part in his life" (308). Information about his birth is said to have come from a journal where he indicates that "he was born in Louisiana, that his mother was Spanish, that he had lived in his extreme youth in Santo Domingo, and that his mother had died there during the Negro insurrection" (309).

Audubon is pictured as a complex figure with quite a struggle establishing himself and his career. As his story evolves, he is shown encountering other bigger-than-life figures of his era, such as Daniel Boone. This seems entirely possible, since Audubon traveled to many places seeking to document nature through his drawings and for his observations of the habitats and developmental habits of birds and animals.

Audubon married Lucy, whom he left behind to raise his children during most of his escapades. Eventually his work is accepted in the upper echelons of the scientific community and he becomes a prominent and prosperous figure.

Even though answers are not clear regarding Audubon's ancestry, many encounters with "Negroes" are described during his travels. Several references are made to "Negroes" being used as oarsmen while traveling through various woods and swamps: "The little party of three made the two day journey by skiff with two Negro oarsmen" (65). He also took seriously the myths told by Negroes about the birds and animals. In New York, he talks to one named Pomp about a bird called "chuck will," which rolls its eggs: "'He roll 'em with his bill. . . . One night I seen him. He mosquito eater. Sometime he swallow little birds whole'" (180). The writer goes on to say, "Sometimes on his longer expeditions he was accompanied by a negro who had been a sailor and could go up a tall cypress as he would climb a mast." Audubon encounters and employs Negroes in many roles. The author speaks of Scipio, "who had only a sheepskin bound by a tight girth for a saddle" and "was an excellent horseman" (99). She continues to describe Scipio killing a bear with an axe.

In Louisiana it is observed that "the Negroes were still close to an ancient primitive life, practicing dark rites in spite of prohibitions and telling stories of birds and animals whose meanings white men could not penetrate." Regarding language, the author describes "African mingling with French to make the soft patois known as creole" (165). Upon the earlier arrival in New Orleans, there is a view of "Negroes, mulattoes, Spaniards, with gold rings in their ears" (147).

In spite of the outdated language and some condescension toward African Americans, there is a lot of useful information here that slight revision would make much more palatable.

(M) *The Codfish Musket* by Agnes Hewes. Doubleday (out of print).

The story begins with Dan Boit watching with a crowd as the *Columbia*, the first American ship to sail around the world, returns to port. It is during this celebration that the only images of African Americans appear—too slight to be important. Regarding part of the celebration at a mansion, it is said, "At the top of the stone steps that led to the mansion stood two Negroes in uniform" (24).

Subsequently, a quite complex story evolves. Dan begins working for a storekeeper and gun dealer. When some firearms are stolen, Dan suspects Tom Gentry, a puzzling Englishman. Much later, Dan is proved right.

Meantime, Dan is sent to Washington in search of rifle customers. While there, he finds a diary belonging to Thomas Jefferson. When he returns the diary, Jefferson is impressed and hires him as his secretary. Later Dan is sent to the Louisiana Territory, just purchased, with a message for Lewis. During his travels the boy uncovers a gang led by Tom Gentry. These culprits are selling guns, including those with the codfish marking, to the British army and Indians. In turn, settlers are being attacked with these guns. The gang's activities are disrupted after this discovery.

(M) *Whistlers' Van* **by Idwal Jones. Viking (out of print).**
Gwilyn has gypsy blood in his veins and the moor road, the road to beyond, has always lured him. That spring when the whistler came, whistling a familiar tune that sounded like a bird, Gwilyn left with him. The story is of the Welsh boy's travels and his win of a big race, which brings him glory. Wales is the setting and the story presents a sympathetic view of gypsy life and lore. No images of Africans are there, but on one occasion Gwilyn is stopped by the constable and told, "We're looking for a pair of Arabs. They're horsemen, they are, and black enough to be Gypsis" (197).

1939

Honor Award

Hello the Boat! **by Phyllis Crawford. Illus. by Edward Laning. Holt (out of print).**
The Doak family, in 1817, travels by boat from Pittsburgh to Cincinnati. There is much fun, adventure, and enjoyment. Within the story of the trip there is mention of a stage performance with music by a Negro orchestra: "The Negroes rolled their eyes and grinned" (164, 168).

Leader by Destiny: George Washington, Man and Patriot **by Jeanette Eaton. Illus. by Jack Manly Rose. Harcourt (out of print).**
It is established early in the story that George Washington was from the upper elite classes. His inheritances are mentioned and also the land owned by his family. His ownership of slaves is very apparent: "A turbaned Negress emerged carrying a tray" (2). There is a quarrel in slave quarters, another negro servant serving food (8), later one chanting (11), and more musicians (30). It is noted that "he recently had bought some promising slaves" (145). Recognition is given to Billy, the devoted slave he brought with him to his new home after marriage (226). Otherwise there is no mention of African Americans as Washington's life story is told.

Revealed is the fact that Washington was smitten with a Sally Fairfax, though he married Martha. They had one child who died. Later, Washington became a general in the American army. Although married and moving on with his life, Washington felt a loss when Sally moved to England.

Of interest is Washington's observation of the Continental Congress Convention. The author notes that ordinary people were not represented but only the elite. Washington witnessed George Mason and Governor Morris as they joined forces "to end the slave trade . . . and plan freedom for the Negroes in bondage." Morris is quoted as saying, "'I will never concur in upholding domestic slavery. It is a nefarious institution. It is the curse of Heaven in states where it prevails.'"

+++*Penn* by Elizabeth Janet Gray. Viking (out of print).

The story of William Penn begins when his father, Captain Penn, returns home to find he has a newborn son, William. Through Penn's life story, we learn of the early origins and suppression of Quakers by the English and French. They are subjected to isolation, rejection, and inquisitions. They immigrate to America.

Although there are not many details, Penn's rejection of slavery is noted when he moves into Pennsbury Manor, where there are three slaves whom he immediately sets free (265). Continuing, Penn attempts to influence the passing of laws against slavery. His actions are said to have taken place eighty years before the Quakers took an official stand against slavery.

1940

Honor Award

Boy with a Pack by Stephen W. Meader. Harcourt (out of print).

Bill sets out to seek his fortune with a peddler's pack upon his back. His story is of various encounters along the way and the necessity to deal with one of the major issues of the time, slavery.

His involvement in the abolition movement and the Underground Railroad is accidental, but he becomes committed to the cause, realizing through his encounters that the people and the issues are very real. The author states, "Bill hadn't given much thought to the slavery question. Like most New Englanders he regarded slave-holding as wrong in principle, but it was a long way off and no particular business of his own" (229).

The boy describes the "colored people," slave and free, whom he meets on his way south: "He had grown used to their funny slurring talk and the mellow huskiness of their voices. They were folks, not so different from white folks" (229).

Bill encounters a horseman named Cawley looking for escaped slaves described as "nigras" and further: "'The man's six foot an' over-a prime field-hand but sulky. Chain scars on his laigs, an' one ear cropped with a "V." No marks on the boy—yet.'"

When Bill seeks shelter with the Halseys, a family of Quakers, he tells them about his encounter with the horseman, not knowing he is at one stop on the Underground Railroad. Someone is encountered in the barn; "a round brown head appeared for an instant." "He caught the flash of scared white eyeballs and then the face was gone." Eben, the Halsey son, explains that the family helps any slaves they can in their struggle to be free. His father had helped a hundred or more escape into Canada with many risks involved and with careful plans made by each Quaker participant. The Halseys were currently hiding the slaves about which Bill had been asked. The escaped father had made a break for it into the woods, but the boy, Banjo, was still in the barn. Eben in his conversation uses the term "darky" to describe the father, showing that those with good intentions maintained negative stereotypes.

Cawley makes a stop at the Halsey home seeking his runaways. After he leaves, the Halseys enlist Bill's aid in transporting Banjo to another location. Bill agrees and carries the boy in a sack, as part of his wares.

Of course, the slave boy's language is dialect: "'Seem lak de stummick gwine jolt out o' me ev'y step.'" The author continues to use the term "darky": "Then he told the small darky exactly what he had to do." Bill is able to deliver the boy safely, though the trip is not easy, with more encounters with Cawley along the way. With a little cleaning up of language, this could be a recommended title.

Runner of the Mountain Tops: The Life of Louis Agassiz by Mabel Robinson. Random House (out of print).
In the author's foreword, it is noted that Louis Agassiz was born in Switzerland, traveled to Germany to study, later went to France and England, and then left for America.

Early in life, it was recognized that Agassiz had an unquenchable thirst for information and knowledge about science. He was sent away to school for access to the best opportunities, and by seventeen he was studying in Zurich. It is said that through his study of nature, botany, and so forth, Agassiz "established the ice age" (152). Many major naturalists and famous scientists of the times are met along the way.

There is no mention of African Americans until late in the book, when the reading of *Uncle Tom's Cabin* is mentioned. The importance of the book's influence on society's views at the time is emphasized (212). Most interesting are the thoughts of Agassiz as a scientist who studied Darwin and others. He believed pure blacks were suited to the South and that mulattos, unpleased with themselves, would die off. The author states that "he looked ahead to a future of rather complete segregation of the races from natural causes." The writer also notes that Agassiz's theories did not prove true. This brief passage strongly endorses the contention that racism was partially formed by inadequate and mistaken science.

1941

Honor Award

(M) *Blue Willow* by Doris Gates. Viking.
Janey Larkin, whose only treasure is a blue willow plate that belonged to her great-great-grandmother, moves with her family from Texas to the San Joaquin Valley in California. A young

Mexican girl, her neighbor, becomes her best friend. This story is a poignant portrayal of life during the years of the dust bowl, when many families experienced fates similar to the Larkins.

Janey and family settle in a small rented shack as her father begins work in the nearby field. Janey's hope is that one day she and her family will have a permanent home. Centering the story is Janey's wish, and scenes of friendship and experiences at school are added.

When Janey's father cannot pay the rent, she offers to give up her treasured blue willow plate. The eventual resolution to the family's problems is positive.

There is only one vision of an African American in the story, which seems almost a mishap. At one point, Janey's father participates in a cotton-picking contest, hoping to win money. The scene is described as follows: "Mr. Larkin was well in the lead of most of the field. Only one man seemed to challenge his chances at first place. This one was a huge Negro whose big black hands moved with unerring deftness and lightning speed." This reference is not necessarily negative, but why was a black person chosen, and why did he have to be the usually *"huge Negro"*? Neither this character nor any other African American character appears anywhere else in the story, and there is no indication that the plight of this person of color could have been *worse* than that of the Larkins.

1942

Newbery Award

(M) *The Matchlock Gun* by Walter D. Edmonds. Dodd, Mead & Co.

It is 1756 when Edward, a ten-year-old boy, saves his family from tribal raids. During the French and Indian War, his father has left home to join the fight. He and the family are told, "If you get lonely, go over to the brick house. It's like a fort and mother has guns for the negroes" (6). The boy meets the challenge of defending the family with a much-too-large Spanish gun his father left. (On pages 17 and 18 the ownership of slaves is very briefly mentioned.)

Honor Award

George Washington's World **by Genevieve Foster. Scribner.**
Foster offers many more details than some about the political life surrounding the rise of George Washington to prominence and about others of his ilk. The author's style of presenting the world stage of the biographee through others of importance may be disconcerting to some, but it is an interesting departure for others.

The slave trade is introduced in a section about John Paul and his experiences as a slaver. Described is the capture of the slaves, the chaining, the groans of "miserable Negroes," and so on. This author, like others, chooses to emphasize the role of African chiefs: "African chieftains were only too ready to sell their subjects for the white trader's rum. They often sent men back in the jungle at night to set fire to the native villages, and capture the terrified creatures as they fled from the flames" (154). Negatives are not balanced by the picture of George Washington returning home and being welcomed by "old Bishop," a slave happy to see him return (248).

Little Town on the Prairie **by Laura Ingalls Wilder. Harper.**
No personal images of African Americans appear in this classic series about Laura and her family, who move to the western prairies. In this one, however, Laura's father participates in a community group. The Literaries are making an attempt to bring art and music to the community. The father joins in a presentation of blackfaced minstrels: "The white circled eyes rolled, the big red mouths blabbed questions and answers that were the funniest ever heard." Then the "five darkies" are described as having raced down the aisle and left, leaving everyone laughing (258, 259). On page 258 of the edition read, a picture of the blackfaced group is shown. Later, Laura notices some strange smudges on her father's face and gets him to confess that "he had been the darky who rattled the bones" (260).

This is an example of how easy it was to place these random negative images in unnecessary places.

1943

Honor Award

(M) *Have You Seen Tom Thumb?* by Mabel Leigh Hunt. Illus. by Fritz Eichenburg. Stokes (out of print).

A long, detailed biography of the little person born Charles Sherwood Stratton reveals a colorful but apparently satisfying life as "Tom Thumb." According to the author's research, P. T. Barnum had a special affection for the child whom he at six dubbed "General Tom Thumb," lying about the boy's age.

The performer's life story takes him to England, where he is received by the queen. His fame travels worldwide. When he comes of age, he marries another little person named Lavinia. The story does not emphasize any of the negatives of his life—no episodes of taunting or hate. Being protected and cared for by Barnum, he feels no sense of rejection. Although some little people now reject the term *midget* used throughout the book, this seems to be an important record of a special person that should be preserved.

When Barnum tells the young boy the story of Aladdin, he says, "'And so the forty white slaves and the forty black ones, all gorgeously robed, went walking' . . . 'The forty black ones looked like forty Colonel Goshens'" (143). Tom Thumb encounters African Americans in New Orleans and upon a visit to Cuba and described very briefly are scenes in which there were slaves and others: "But, he liked Havana, its blue and red houses, its slim dark little men, its plump dark little women." In the next paragraph he admires the "Negro postilions, all silver and lace from chin to waist" (200).

(M) *The Middle Moffat* by Eleanor Estes. Harcourt.

These humorous stories of the Moffats contain no African American characters. Why do authors of such single-culture material choose to throw in inferences that could only be interpreted as derogatory? In this story, the children are looking through a batch of books and find some mostly about missionaries among cannibals with an illustration titled "Zulu Chief" (31). Later, Joey is fascinated by and learns to play the organ. He plays by ear "My Country 'Tis of Thee" and "Old Black Joe." The latter title is mentioned several times (38–39).

1944

Newbery Award

Johnny Tremain **by Esther Forbes. Houghton.**

Johnny, who wishes to be a master silversmith, works for Mr. Lapham, who needs the boy to keep him organized. An African is introduced early in the story when Mr. Hancock comes to visit and place an order: "Close to the door was a tiny African holding a slender gray horse by the bridle" (19). Johnny Tremain speaks to the boy and the African answers: "'Oh, no sir,' said little Jehu, *rolling his eyes*" (20). Later Jehu is referred to as "that dressed up doll of a black boy" (61).

The boy's story proceeds through the streets of Boston, his competition for the best place of apprenticeship, and encounters with the growing political intrigue. Others of African descent are met. On one occasion, a black girl threw some dirty dishwater out a window without seeing Johnny and soaked him. Johnny's reaction was, "If he had not counted ten, he would have told her what he thought of her, black folk in general." The girl apologizes using soft dialect: "'Oh little master, I'se so sorry! Now you just step right into de kitchen and I'll dry up them close'"(109).

Johnny elicits the help of Lydia, "the handsome black washerwoman of the inn" (153). To save his horse Goblin from being taken by the British, Lydia flaps a sheet at the right moment, spooking the horse. She also reports to Johnny about the British army's activities. Her dialect is soft: "'And dat dere Lieutenant Stranger, he was standin' by de fireplace'" (195). Tremain's interactions with Lydia continue through several pages and none of the hostility shown to the other servant appears. She is referred to on at least two occasions as a "handsome black laundress."

Tremain is involved with Paul Revere, Dr. Warren, and others planning a revolt. Warren has a black servant referred to as "his colored man" (228). The story continues introducing young readers to possible scenarios dramatizing the formation of early American history with emphasis on the Boston Tea Party. This title is not as deeply marred as several others written during this period.

1945

Honor Award

Abraham Lincoln's World by Genevieve Foster. Scribner (out of print).

As in her previous book about George Washington, Foster offers much more than biography. As Lincoln is profiled, many details about historical developments in Europe as they affect the climate in America are provided.

In her typical fashion, Foster builds a biography through views of other historical persons and events prominent at the time. Done in conversational style, this approach is similar to attempts at history such as that of van Loon in *The Story of Mankind*. Some will find this approach useful.

Facts about slavery are interspersed, though no Africans or African Americans are among the characters personified. Garrison and Harriet Beecher are mentioned in relationship to the abolitionist movement, but not Frederick Douglass (151). "'Darkest Africa' it was called when David Livingston was moved to go to the great continent" begins a short narrative about Livingston (165). Several pages document the debates about slave states and free states (232–235). More is written about Harriet Beecher Stowe's production of *Uncle Tom's Cabin* (236–237); Lincoln's attitudes toward slavery and the debates with Douglas (268–271); and Lincoln's commitment to and writing of the Emancipation Proclamation (307–309). Frederick Douglass is mentioned as one of the persons watching as Lincoln makes his second inaugural speech (328).

1946

Newbery Award

(M) *Strawberry Girl* by Lois Lenski. Lippincott.
This is not a strawberry-picking story as may be indicated by the title; instead, readers face major conflicts between two families. The Boyers have just moved to Florida from North Carolina to raise strawberries and other produce. The Slaters, who raise cattle, are longtime residents of the area. The cattle-raising family resists building fences and allows their cattle to invade other peoples' farms nearby, especially the land of the Boyers. Hostility grows and violence ensues between the two families. Killing each other's animals is one final tactic. Lessons in the futility of violence may have been the selection committee's focus.

There are no significant images of African Americans, though mention is made: "Sometimes Negroes in wagons rode by on their way to the turpentine" (74). On a visit to the depot, "Old Simon, a crippled colored man" is noted (123).

Honor Award

New Found World by Katherine Shippen. Viking (out of print).
Limited histories for young people about the historical development of Latin America are available. Although dated, this book provides some basic information about Portuguese and Spanish explorers and early developments in Latin America. An update might be useful.

There is discussion of Haiti in a section titled "Tropical Storms in the Caribbean." In a chapter titled "Brazil Breaks Away from Portugal," the presence of Africans is mentioned: "In the north were large plantations where Negroes worked under a few white men. The climate made both blacks and whites lazy and indolent" (197).

1948

Honor Award

The Cow-Tail Switch and Other West African Stories by Harold Courlander. Holt.

The author has collected West African tales, many of which are very suitable for retelling. Some cultural information is provided as in the title story; the switch made from a cow's tail is used to fan flies.

(M) *Pancakes-Paris* by Claire Huchet Bishop. Viking (out of print).

A young boy from a French family tells the story of life after World War II. A widowed mother struggles to keep her family intact and fed, when along come two American soldiers, who become part of the family. Charles and Zezette are living a frugal life when Charles is given a box from which he is supposed to make crepes, but directions on the box are in English. Charles hides the box, hoping to find out how to make the crepes and present a surprise for his mother and sister. There is a picture of a "nice negro lady on the box." Charles dreams of the lady and in illustration we see Aunt Jemima.

The boy wanders around the city seeking help with the box directions. He asks a Negro porter and finally a lady who explains how to make pancakes from the box. Two soldiers hear his story and give him a ride home. The next day the soldiers return, bringing the family a feast, and they make the pancakes.

1949

Newbery Award

(M) *King of the Wind* by Marguerite Henry. Rand McNally.

Agba, a mute Moroccan boy, is designated to care for and deliver an Arabian horse, Sham, to King Louis the XV. After experiencing many mishaps the boy delivers the horse, now thin and ravaged. The once powerful Sham is reduced to pulling a cart, but eventually he and his loving caretaker live at the great estate called Godolphin. Here, Sham becomes sire of the Godolphin lineage, which is ancestral to today's thoroughbreds. The story is highly fictionalized but provides much information for horse lovers.

Honor Award

(M) *Seabird* **by Holling C. Holling. Houghton.**
A seagoing boy fills his time by carving a seabird. Ezra keeps the bird with him at all times as he journeys around the world. The seabird becomes his good luck piece, which is passed down from generation to generation. The carving is the basis for this series of short stories that follow seafaring, exploration, and the developments therein over several generations. The reader learns of journeys across the oceans of the world. Contained are illustrations and sketches.

One note about Doc, "the Negro cook," appears on page 26. He is pictured in an illustration. We learn little about him except "he hated cold," and between meals he stoked the fires.

+++*Story of the Negro* by Arna Bontemps. Knopf (out of print).
Bontemps presents an extremely objective view of historical developments surrounding African Americans from Africa to the civil rights era in America. Here is much information not to be found in other historical materials, especially during this period.

1950

Honor Award

Tree of Freedom **by Rebecca Caudill. Viking (out of print).**
Kentucky was far away from the major fighting in the Revolutionary War. This story, told through the eyes of Stephanie, a young girl, speaks to the effects of the war on this place apart. The details and descriptions of time and place are very interesting. The

colloquial Kentucky hill language is not unpleasant but may be awkward for young people.

At one point there is discussion about Marguerite de Monchard's experiences in Charleston. She talks about "a big Gambian Negro standing chained on the auction block. The Gambian was as strong as a brute ox for field labor, barked the auctionee." (88). Marguerite shouts her protest about this horror and her family is chased from the area. The discussion continues for a couple of pages. After hearing this story, Stephanie plants a seed for a "tree of freedom." The apple tree seed is dug up and eaten by a chicken. In an unlikely scene, Stephanie operates on the chicken and retrieves the seed, replants it, and it grows.

1951

Newbery Award

Amos Fortune, Free Man by Elizabeth Yates. Dutton.

This fictionalized biography is of a person about whom little is known. Yates has fashioned a world around Fortune, attempting to tell the story of one slave from capture to old age.

The main character, whose African name, At-mun, was changed to Amos, was captured at the age of fifteen just as he was participating in celebrations of transition to adulthood. He is said to have been a prince and, during the terrible passage to America, tried to remember his past and take pride in it. Instead of facing the horrible situations of slavery experienced by most, Amos is bought by a Quaker named Caleb and lives a relatively easy life. Caleb gives the slave his freedom, but Amos refuses to leave. After Caleb dies, Amos is sold to another fairly easy master who is a tanner and teaches him the trade. Later, Amos is able to buy his freedom and set up his own tanning business in New Hampshire.

Some indicators of the difficulties faced in white society are shown in various scenes, such as when a buyer simply refuses to pay the promised amount for a tanning job and laughs. There is nothing Amos can do about it.

Amos is portrayed as a gentle, loving, religious man with little anger regarding his situation in life. He maintains positive feelings about himself and his past life. There is the remnant of a love story in the end when he seeks out the woman he admires, buys her freedom, and marries her. Apparently, he is credited with having bought the freedom of others.

Very few aesthetic comments are provided. Some scenes present stereotypical images of blacks preferring white, as in one scene when Amos gives Celyndia a doll made from cornstalks, with a face painted on leather. The author states, in the previous paragraph, "White was the most beautiful color she knew." Amos reminds the child that the brown of the earth is a good color too. Later the author states that Celyndia, holding the doll, "hugged her *dusky* baby." She had wanted a dollie with "a white china face and pretty pink cheeks." The author *does* say Celyndia loves the doll *because Amos made it for her*, not because she finds the doll beautiful.

There are the usual condescending references toward African Americans, such as, "'But that's what they are, those black people, nothing but children. It's a good thing for them the whites took them over.'" Readers are left to decide if the negative social situations and conversations are products of the times, rather than perceptions of truth.

Honor Award

Abraham Lincoln, Friend of the People by Clare Ingram Judson. Follett (out of print).

Judson's focus is on the early life of this popular president. Information about the politics of the presidency is sparse. Slavery and the Emancipation Proclamation, of course, are covered.

Gandhi, Fighter without a Sword by Jeanette Eaton. Morrow (out of print).

Although designed for the young, this is a powerful presentation of the amazing legendary figure. Eaton emphasizes the far-reaching nature of Gandhi's influence during his times. The negative aspects of colonial attitudes are clear. When Mohandas traveled to South Africa to fight for the rights of Indian workers, he encountered prejudices similar to those imposed on Africans. Indians were subject to being called names like "coolie and "sammie." "In the white man's eyes Indians stood a little higher than the native Negroes. At least they were allowed to vote for Assembly members and negroes had no vote of any kind. But the English and Dutch descendants who ran South African affairs could make no further distinctions among dark-skinned people" (48). In Pretoria, Gandhi seeks a hotel and meets a soft-spoken Negro who says to him, "'I'm an American. If you are alone here, I'll guide you to a hotel owned by an American.'" He does, but even there Gandhi is told that because of the attitude of Europeans, he is not allowed to eat in the dining room.

Gandhi's continuing nonviolent and famous crusade was for the rights of Indians and did not concern itself with Africans and African Americans, but the author takes time to show similarities in the plight of all "dark" peoples.

1952

Newbery Award

(M) *Ginger Pye* **by Eleanor Estes. Harcourt.**

Readers visit Cranbury, Connecticut, during 1924. When Jerry Pye purchases a dog, someone follows him as he takes the dog home. Together Jerry and his three-year-old Uncle Bennie name the dog "Ginger" because it is the color of ginger and has a spicy personality.

Soon thereafter, the dog is missing. Everyone in the community helps to search for the dog, but all seems lost. Jerry and Uncle Bennie do not readily give up the hunt. After approximately ten months, Uncle Bennie finds the dog, Ginger Pye, which had been kidnapped by Bullwinkle, one of Jerry's classmates.

As with many titles in the Newbery collection, this one contains no significant images of Africans or African Americans. At least one passage could be considered unsavory. Rachel has been stung by a bee and her bottom lip has swollen. She says, "Ubangi," when looking at herself in the mirror and remembering some pictures seen at school. The passage, which continues for only a few sentences, is intended to be funny, but probably not to Ubangis (82).

Honor Award

(M) *Minn of the Mississippi* by Holling C. Holling. Houghton.

Minn, a great three-legged snapping turtle, travels down the Mississippi River. The sights and sounds of the lands and people are chronicled. There is much to learn here about geography, history, and geology, especially in the maps and illustrations provided in the margins.

In an overall positive presentation, African Americans are encountered in the section "Land of Cotton and Turtle Stew." They are also pictured in color illustrations (68–71). Though the illustrations are not unattractive, like the verbalizations found in other places, the artist paints some of those local characters with somewhat large popping eyes. Stories are told about the capture and escape of the turtle. A sampling of African American verbalizations follow. In Memphis, Tennessee, Minn pauses to view the cotton fields: "A white haired Negro talked with the tourists [with a soft dialect], 'like in de song, No suh.' . . . 'She growed corn and taters.' . . . 'Dis river, he seen me grow strong'" (68). There is balance provided when a local Caucasian boy also speaks in local dialect.

1956

Newbery Award

(M) *Carry On, Mr. Bowditch* by Jean Lee Latham. Houghton.

Nathaniel Bowditch has always been fascinated with astronomy, the stars, and mathematics. He learned Latin so that he could read Newton's *Principia*, about astronomy. Bowditch becomes a master of figures and gains expert knowledge of the stars. After serving as an apprentice, he goes to sea, where the captain is more than impressed with his navigational skills. With his knowledge, Bowditch is able to navigate the ship through a terrible storm and on his last voyage brings the ship safely into harbor on a very foggy evening. Nat Bowditch taught others and wrote *The American Practical Navigator*, used by seamen everywhere.

On the ship there is one African American character: "Even Herbie, the huge Negro cook, wanted to hear Mr. Bowditch talk about the stars." Herbie speaks, "'Doggone . . . it kind of picks a fellow up to think about the stars. Kind of makes you forget about soaking the salt beef till its fitten to eat. . . . Just think of me learning things! Me!'" (110).

Bowditch does not find it easy to teach. He has to learn how to state things that are easy for him understand more simply for the learner. This leads to the keeping of a notebook of lessons, which he uses later.

Earlier in the story, when Bowditch is being recruited for his tenure on the ship, he listens to a Mr. Derby give instructions to Captain Prince, "'There are only two things I expressly forbid. You'll never break the law of any port you enter, And you'll never—*never* enter into the slave trade.' . . . 'I'd rather lose any ship I own than to have it become a slaver! There is no excuse that I'd accept. Even if a slaver attacked you, overpowered you, and ordered you to carry a cargo of slaves—even that would be no excuse! You'd go down fighting—but you wouldn't turn a Derby ship into a slaver!'" Unconsciously Nat claps his hands (100–101). Unobtrusively, the author makes a positive statement against slavery.

1957

Honor Award

***Mr. Justice Holmes* by Clara Ingram Judson. Illus. by Robert Todd. Follett (out of print).**

A lot of information about the chief justice and his times is included in this biography for young people. The privileged background and upbringing of Oliver Wendell Holmes Jr. are clearly delineated, as the author provides information about his early schooling and early influences on his life. Holmes does not have a very good relationship with his father, whose life is focused on being famous while young Wendell is becoming fascinated with the law. Holmes goes to Harvard, then enlists in the military during the Civil War, to the consternation of his father. Their relationship is repaired somewhat when young Holmes is wounded. His father travels in search of his son to bring him home for healing. Upon return to the war, young Holmes advances in military station, but when the war is over, he has decided to go to law school.

He later marries and slowly advances in his profession. Holmes makes a name for himself through writing a book and through hard work and enlightened opinions on the bench.

The images of African Americans here are only through discussions of the laws regarding runaways, abolition, and so on. These issues are given several pages as background to Holmes's commitment to Lincoln and to identify his philosophical background, but no African American persons are identified except in newspaper articles.

1958

Newbery Award

Rifles for Watie by Harold V. Keith. Crowell.

Another of the award-winning books dealing with the Civil War is this one starring Jeff, who lives with his family in Kansas Territory. Jeff joins the Union Army and is led by Captain Asa Clardy. He soon meets with the captain's mean disposition. Eventually, near the end of the story, Clardy is found to be a traitor and has to run away. He has been trading rifles to the enemy.

Jeff meets a young female supporter of the Confederacy when he and his company stop at her house to demand food. He learns later from a "Negro passing by" that the girl is daughter of Levi Washbourne, captain of the Confederate Cherokee Cavalry. Immediately becoming smitten with the girl, Jeff attempts to show that he is a gentleman by doing chores for the house. This relationship is a subplot; primarily emphasis is on the tough life of the infantry and the hunger and fatigue encountered.

Mixed inferences are contained in the presentation of African Americans. In one case the regiment stops in a town and "they ran into a Negro who had emerged from a deserted brick store, carrying a large ham." *Again*, "the whites of his eyes rolled in fright" (149). Later Jeff is stopped by a Negro slave who asks him if he would please come to his cabin. There another is dying and has prayed to live long enough to see a "'Linkum soldier.'" "'It he last chance, young massa,'" says the slave (154). Jeff enters the poorly furnished place and sees the old man whose black skin is "wrinkled like parchment paper." When the man sits up and sees Jeff in uniform, he says, "'I bress God,'" falls back, and dies. Jeff was told that the old man was probably more than one hundred years old. An old woman Jeff meets talks about people who owned "niggers" and treated them well (161).

Upon meeting Lucy again, Jeff discusses the reasons for the war. When she asks why they make war upon the South, Jeff answers, "'Many think we make war upon the South for the sole purpose of restoring the Union. I know slavery's involved too.'" He goes on to explain that Lincoln had not planned to interfere with slavery.

Following are some of the references to African Americans found as Jeff continues his involvement in the war. In one conversation, David says, "'An the rebels will sass us riht back by askin' us if the niggers we are fightin' for have improved the Yankee breed'" (188). Near a church, Jeff meets a Negro boy, "a sweat rag tied around his head." Jeff asks him why the graveyards are always near the church. The boy answers, "'So the dead folks can heah the organ music an' the singin' on Sundays, I reckon'" (238). There is a long conversation between the two concerning the boy serving in the Yankee army. Jeff sends a message to the fort by the boy, who does join the army. Later, Jeff becomes sick and awakens at the home of the Jackmans, being served by "a Negro woman, huge and billowy, her shining, blue-black hair bound in a red handkerchief, [who] waddled into the room. . . . When she opened her vast mouth to grin at him, her teeth reminded Jeff of row of white piano keys." Jeff seeks for Lucy again at her home, but a Negro woman answers the door, saying, "'Naw suh! She's gone down to Mary's to rub her mothah's back.'" The term "negress" is used to refer to the servant woman. "Her friendliness made him feel good all over" (222). The woman converses with him in soft dialect, telling him how she arrived at the home of the Jackmans. The added wartime complexity of tribal groups owning slaves is interjected when the Jackmans and Hannah are attacked by the Pin Tribe. There are many more references to African Americans—too long to quote here.

In the appended notes, it is said that the story was the result of the author's study of Civil War records, histories, letters of the Cherokees, and more. It is regrettable that this historical novel with good background information is overbearing in its presentation of African Americans, even though some of the references may be considered appropriate to the times. Some of the negative descriptions originate with the author, such as the one mentioned above with the woman having a "vast mouth." He also repeats the cliché of "eyes rolling" several times. It reads as if Africans had some affliction that allowed their eyes to roll around in their heads at will.

Honor Award

(M) *Gone-Away Lake* by Elizabeth Enright. Harcourt.

Eleven-year-old Portia Blake and her brother, Foster, six years old, travel for the first time without their parents. By train they visit their cousin Julian.

Portia and Julian explore and play together and while walking through a forest discover the remnants of an old resort community near a bog. The two children meet and become friends with this area's only two inhabitants. From them, stories are heard about the past when the bog was a lake, the gone-away lake.

No images of people of African descent appear, but there is one questionable short passage in which a boxer dog is described: "Her face looked like a very dark, sad person's face attached to a dog." It continues, explaining that Portia is fond of imagining that the dog "was a real person who had been enchanted into a dog: a princess, or *little girl from Africa*" (10).

(M) *The Great Wheel* by Robert Lawson. Viking.
Cornelius (Conn), at the age of eighteen, leaves Ireland and travels to America. We follow his fortunes as he becomes involved in the construction of the first Ferris wheel at the Chicago World's Fair, 1893. There are many descriptions of life at the time and many details of the atmosphere and vast scale of preparation for the fair. Ferris's dream of "the wheel" is realized; it becomes one of the focal aspects of the exhibition: "The cars were lighted . . . the huge wheel was the most conspicuous feature." Cornelius helps with the handling of passengers.

There are few references to African Americans, but describing the pending setting for the Midway, Conn's Uncle Patrick describes, "'Villages of every variety of strange and savage . . . Japanese, Filipinos, Indians, Fijis, Egyptians.'" In one brief mention, "the Negro fireman dozed" (135). On one night "a group of Negroes," described as Pullman porters and other workers from the railroad station or waiters from nearby, were making their way home. When seeing the wheel, they broke into song, singing the spiritual "Ezekiel Saw the Wheel" (140–141). So often the only mention of African Americans is as singers, which in itself is not negative, but contributes to an overall stereotype of happy singing slaves and, in this case, happy singing workers.

Tom Paine, Freedom's Apostle by Leo Gurko. Crowell (out of print).
Although simply written, the complexities of this important historical figure are revealed. His publications, including *Rights of Man* and *Age of Reason*, are classics still analyzed in social studies and history classes. The author of this biography makes his life abroad and in America accessible to the young. He is included in this list not as an abolitionist but as one who wrote about issues at the center of the idea of slavery, especially in the *Rights of Man*.

The author credits Paine with having written the "first proclamation of Negro emancipation," in Pennsylvania (90).

1959

Newbery Award

***The Witch of Blackbird Pond* by Elizabeth George Speare. Houghton.**
Rachel was born on Barbados but after being orphaned ends up residing in a Puritan household in Connecticut. Here, she meets a Quaker woman named Hannah, who lives apart from the rest of the community. Some say she is a witch. Rachel establishes a relationship with the woman, visits her often, and soon finds herself also accused. The story follows Rachel's attempts to adjust to her new life situation, her struggles with the rigidity of Puritanism, her defense against accusations of witchcraft, and her development of a love relationship.

In the beginning it is established that Rachel comes from a rich family that owned plantations in Barbados. When asked by John what happened to her after her parents' death and if there were women to care for her, she says, "'Oh, slaves of course. I had a black nurse'" (19). In one passage she discusses slavery with another character, Nat. He asks, "'I suppose you never knew about slaves on Barbados?'" Her answer, "'Of course I knew. We own—we used to own—more than a hundred. How else could you work a plantation?'" Nat then asks, "'Did you think they traveled from Africa in private cabins like yours?'" (23). On a third occasion, Kit, in discussion with Matt and Rachel, talks about having to sell all the land and the slaves and having to sell her own "'Negro girl.'" She refers to "the little African slave who had been her shadow for twelve years" (37). Cousin Judith quips about Kit, "'Will she expect us all to wait on her hand and foot like her black slaves?'" (49). Kit also sees black faces that "must be slaves" at her first church service (53). There are no fleshed-out African American characters in the story, only these references apparently designed to emphasize Kit's privileged upbringing and lack of sensitivity about slavery.

1960

Newbery Award

(M) *Onion John* by Joseph Krumgold. Crowell.

Societal lessons are soon to be learned when young Andy Rusch befriends the unusual resident of their town called Onion John. John is a European immigrant who lives in a hut filled with bathtubs in which he grows onions and eats them like apples. The man is happy with his life, having plenty to eat and plenty of cast-off clothing. Once in a while, money is earned by doing odd jobs for his neighbors.

Matters become complicated when Andy's father decides that John should have a real home and convinces the town to support him in building one. Disaster happens almost immediately after John moves in. Not used to modern life, he leaves a newspaper on the stove and the new house burns. Onion John leaves town frustrated by the interference and the attempted control of his life. Andy, of course, is saddened and tries to make his friend change his mind.

A comment about Africans briefly appears when a young friend reports to Andy his father's words used to solicit the town's support for building John's new home: "'Your father talked of the *Umbangis*' . . . 'how we send billions of dollars all over the world trying to civilize the *Umbangis* and natives like that!' . . . 'We ought to do the same for Onion John.'" This is the second Newbery title that makes fun of the African tribe.

Honor Award

***America Is Born: A History for Peter* by Gerald W. Johnson. Illus. by Leonard Everett Fisher. Morrow.**

A personalized history of the times between Columbus's adventures and 1787 in America is told in this volume. The facts are humanized by the author's translation of important persons' thoughts and feelings.

Very little is included about African Americans, but the author states, "The ones who had the most conspicuous and most lasting effect on the country did not come on their own free will." The paragraph continues with information about a Dutch ship that arrives in Jamestown in 1619 *before* the *Mayflower*. The Dutch sold commodities including "'twenty negurs'" (169). The next page discusses slavery, saying many thought there was nothing wrong with it, "but it was a great crime." The discussion proceeds briefly.

Fisher's illustrations are stark, but the ones of African slaves border on being gross (170–171).

1962

Newbery Award

The Bronze Bow by Elizabeth George Speare. Houghton.

Set in biblical times, *The Bronze Bow* takes place during the Roman occupation of Israel. After losing both his mother and father to horrors of Roman occupation, Daniel holds overwhelming hatred and vows revenge. The story follows Daniel's life in servitude and his involvement with rebel groups trying to fight back against the Romans. Meantime, he falls in love with Thacia.

The group of rebels captures a black slave: "He walked up to the slave and clapped a hand on the trunklike forearm. His own powerful body was dwarfed beside that of his prisoner." The group laugh in their conversation about the slave, calling him "Samson" and "Goliath." Because the slave does not speak, they think he might be deaf and "'dumb too, I wager. Lots of those black ones are mutes.'" The slave becomes a *loyal* servant.

Honor Award

(M) Frontier Living by Edwin Tunis. World.

Tunis capsules America's early history by concentrating on the way people lived, worked, and traveled. Interspersed are notes about the political realities of the times. Also, illustrations help viewers realize how houses, cabins, and local topography appeared.

Very little mention is made of African Americans, except in one section called "Beyond The Mississippi." Most of those references regard the political handling of slavery. The Northwest Ordinance of 1787, which forbade slavery north of the Ohio, is noted as the chapter begins (97). In another section titled "Other Boats," French planters moved their goods in a big bateau steered by the owner "from beneath a regal canopy . . . rowed by eight or ten Negro slaves" (67). On page 99, brief mention is made about the controversy about slavery and Texas's annexation.

This is a book that could be referenced for small details about frontier living. Profuse illustrations and notes cover a numbers of topics like soddies, trails, trading, freight, mail, and much more.

1963

Honor Award

Men of Athens **by Olivia Coolidge. Houghton (out of print).**

Information in this title is still pertinent to the study of ancient Greece. The portrayal of life during these times seems accurate. These stories begin in 496 BC. In a chapter about King Xerxes seeking contributing warriors from every part of his empire, the author writes, "there were Ethiopians in leopard skins carrying Stone Age weapons. . . . There were hook-nosed Easterners with olive complexions, brown men, black men, red haired, blue-eyed men" (28). Throughout the stories there is discussion of slavery, but readers become aware that the system of slavery was totally different from the American system. Stories end with the death of the Golden Age.

1964

Newbery Award

(M) *It's Like This, Cat* **by Emily Neville. Illus. by Emil Weiss. Harper.**

Dave, a fourteen-year-old New York City boy, is alienated from his father and suffers some of the usual adolescent problems with school, self-esteem, and girls. When the boy adopts a stray tomcat, his life begins to change. Talking to his new companion allows Dave to face his problems, real and imagined. In Dave's travels and adventures throughout the city, there are no views or encounters with African Americans except, by assumption, the janitor of his building. This can be assumed by the type of dialect assigned to the janitor, which is the kind relegated to blacks: "'Yas'm,' said Butch. He says 'Yas'm' to all ladies" (4). The text never says Butch is African American.

1965

Honor Award

+++*Across Five Aprils* by Irene Hunt. Follett.

Although no Africans or African Americans are presented in this compelling story about a community facing the complexities of the Civil War, attitudes toward slaves and slavery are contributed through the characters and their conversations. One character named Wilse questions his cousin John, an abolitionist, "'Ain't there been slavery from the beginning of history?'" He admits owning slaves and also questions why, if slavery was wrong, did leaders who shaped the Constitution recognize slavery. Continuing, Wilse asks, "'If tomorrow every slave in the South had his freedom and come up North, would you abolitionists fit the crocodile tears sloshed out of their eyes so they could take the black man by the hand?'" He wants to know if Blacks will be invited to their homes, churches, and schools.

Jethro, the nine-year-old main character, hears these conversations and is troubled by it all, including what real fighting entails. His older brother, Bill, is equally troubled. After Jethro is awakened by a nightmare, Bill comforts him and they discuss the war. Bill states, "'I hate slavery, Jeth, but I hate another slavery of people workin' their lives away in dirty factories for a wage.'"

Other aspects of war and politics are interjected. Ross Milton, a newspaper editor, speaks to Jethro: "'There will be men and women with dark faces who will walk the length and width of this land in search of the bright promise the thirteenth amendment holds for them.'"

Most importantly, the story confronts the conflicts in Jethro's family as brothers consider and take different paths. Through their decisions to participate in the war, readers can assume that this kind of family conflict happened many times during this critical period in American history.

1966

Newbery Award

+++*I, Juan de Pareja* by Elizabeth Borton de Trevino. Farrar.

This is one of the best portrayals of persons of African descent in the Newbery collection. Set in the early seventeenth century, this is the story of Juan de Pareja, born in Seville, Spain. In this version of his life Juan is described as a slave, though in other reference books, he is called a servant. His life and struggles are artfully presented.

Juan dreams of being an artist and as the slave-servant of Diego Velasquez, he masters painting. The relationship between the two is one of friendship, though lines of master and servant are clearly delineated. There are many sources available for more detailed information about Pareja's life, but this is certainly a suitable introduction.

Descriptors are positive. When Pareja meets a girl with whom he falls in love, he describes her: "'a girl about my own age, delicately pale and dainty but with large dark eyes and tightly curling hair of my race'" (69) and more, "an African in all her beauty, had lived among Arab people" (69). It probably was easier for this author to positively describe a light-skinned person of African descent.

When Juan and his beloved Lolis are eventually freed, they discuss slavery. She speaks, "'I resented being bound, I know that God made us all free and that no man should own another. . . . I hated being owned! It was all I could do, some days, to keep the hot words inside my mouth.'"

At the end, about Pareja and Velasquez, the author states, "These two, who began in youth as master and slave, continued as companions in their maturity and ended as equals and friends."

Honor Award

The Noonday Friends by Mary Stolz. Harper.

Set in New York City, two girls form a friendship and give readers a view of an immigrant neighborhood. Franny and Simone, who is Puerto Rican, are friends. They share lunch together and spend time discussing the usual things girls do. In addition, there are the family troubles. Franny's father has job problems and so does Simone's family. There is not much money to spend. At one point, when someone in Simone's family gets a job and his paintings exhibited, Franny and friend have a quarrel and do not speak to each other, but the spat ends happily.

No African Americans are verbally identified, but the pictures show that one of three boys, including Franny's brother, who collect bottles to return for cash is African American.

1967

Honor Award

+++*The Jazz Man* by Mary H. Weik. Atheneum.

Illustrated with striking, attractive woodcuts, this slim volume presents a young boy who has just moved to New York City with his parents. Because he is crippled in one foot and leg, the boy stays at home during the day, spending most of his time dreaming and looking out the window. He becomes familiar with everyone who lives behind windows within view. Especially fascinating to him is the beginning of activity behind one window, formerly vacant, with rooms painted yellow. The new tenant enters with the big box that we soon learn is a piano. Now the boy focuses his attention on watching and listening to the "Jazz Man." Suddenly, there are the surprising occurrences of the boy's mother leaving, his father leaving, and the boy almost starving in the house alone. Happily, these events are only a dream.

The author writes the story in almost poetic tones, especially when she speaks about the jazz man's music: "He could play your mama's worries right out of her head, when the rent man was nagging her for the rent money she didn't have. He could play the sad look off her mouth, and shiny silver slippers onto her feet." These passages also alert readers to the possibilities of family troubles. Further on she writes, "He could play your Daddy out of his no-job blues." The author captures just enough of city flavors to entice the reader and adds elements of pathos and a harsher reality through the dream. Skillfully done.

1968

Honor Award

+++*The Egypt Game* by Zilpha Keatley Snyder. Atheneum.

April and her African American friend Dorothea discover a perfect setting to play their Egypt game. A fenced-in lot in the back of an antique store becomes the backdrop for setting up Egyptian shrines and performing daily rituals. Dorothea's young brother, who is always in her care, is the third character in play. Matters of race are unobtrusive to the story, and this time, the author presents an interracial friendship that seems as real as any others. There are a couple of humorous, childlike passages where the issues of race appear. April's grandmother says, "'Mrs. Ross teaches school and her husband is a graduate student at the university. . . . They're African Americans.'" April replies, "'Dorothea and I know a lot of black people. There are a lot of black people in show business'" (13).

The professor, who owns the back lot that the girls have chosen, sees the Egypt game's developments through a window but does not reveal himself. He describes the group as they enter the area through a hole in the fence. Of April, he states, "Her high cheekbones and short nose were spattered with freckles and there was a strange droopy look to her eyes" (6). April loves to wear false eyelashes, which sometimes become askew. Of Dorothea he says, "The other girl . . . was African American, as was the little boy himself. A similarity in their pert features and slender eyebrows indicated that they were probably brother and sister" (6). No attempts at color descriptions are made.

A rather light, funny mystery develops as more participants are added to the creativity of the Egypt game.

+++*Jennifer, Hecate, Macbeth, William McKinley, and Me, Elizabeth* by E. L. Konigsburg. Atheneum.

This delightful story transmits African American images, which the reader only realizes from the pictures. Sadly, the illustrations, probably intended to be humorous, are unappealing and not too clear. The main character, Elizabeth, describes her new friend Jennifer as a young eccentric. Elizabeth is an only child, is new in town, and walks home from school through the woods, where she discovered Jennifer in a tree. Across the street from this area is a farm and a caretaker's house.

There are many things Elizabeth does not understand about Jennifer, who describes herself as a witch and proceeds to use ritual and verse to prove it. For example, early in the story when the two go trick-or-treating together, "she [Jennifer] opened her bag, stuck her head down inside, and said:

'Bag, sack, parcel post,
Fill thyself
With goodies most.'"

Jennifer proceeds to teach Elizabeth how to be a witch. Elizabeth has assignments to do all week and the two meet at the library, go to the park, and practice their rituals. Eventually trouble ensues.

As indicated earlier there is no mention of African Americans or Africa, except one very brief passage, when Elizabeth says, "Even in Africa where there are plenty of witches called witch doctors" (67).

There have been many objections to this book by those who oppose the use of witchcraft as a theme, but it is mostly a funny story about friends interacting and learning about each other.

1969

Honor Award

+++*To Be A Slave* by Julius Lester. Dial.

Julius Lester begins his book with his own definition of slavery, followed by pages of selected notes, records, and letters of ex-slaves from the Library of Congress. Pertinent to the discussion here, near the end of his introductory comments, Lester states, "Yet slaves are pictured as little more than dumb, brute animals, whose sole attributes were found in working, singing, and dancing" (29).

Lester allows slaves to tell their own story through the narratives with defining comments by the author interspersed. Displayed is a verbal picture of human beings sometimes facing desperate times and horrible brutality. Some selected notes help the reader understand individual methods of coping with these horrors. Many of the Newbery selections have characters who are slaves presented as caricatures of themselves. These narratives speak volumes in correcting some of those images.

1970

Newbery Award

Sounder by William H. Armstrong. Harper.

This selection caused much consternation in the African American community of librarians and reviewers, along with others. Offered here is an often poignant story of a poor African American boy in the South, whose father is a sharecropper. Father struggles to feed his family and on one occasion returns home with a ham. He is soon arrested for stealing the ham and taken to jail. Later he serves on the chain gangs that were common at the time. Sounder is the coon dog that has been the father's constant companion for years.

When the boy is sent to visit his father in jail, the cake he carries is crumbled in the search for contraband. Later, the boy travels alone seeking the chain gang with which his father is serving. Father serves his time and returns home, maimed and devoid of any zest for life. He eventually dies. There is little dialect used, just attempts to capture the local vernacular, by using words like "aint." Most of the early controversy surrounded the author's decision to give only the dog a name. Maybe his intention was to present this family as a generic group representing many, but for a community seeking representation in the literature, personal humanity was at stake. Authors and readers were begging for the authenticity of writings by African Americans. It was strongly felt that children, being exposed to literature about African Americans for the first time, should experience the pain of such experiences through the eyes, ears, and feelings of those who knew it personally.

1972

Honor Award

+++*The Planet of Junior Brown* by Virginia Hamilton. Macmillan.

Readers will rarely find characters as intriguing as those found here. In this outstanding novel about life in the city, Junior Brown is a three-hundred-pound boy who loves the piano. He will do anything to learn to play the piano well, including practice without a piano. Junior's friend Buddy is a street-savvy young man whose mission is to provide havens in deserted buildings called "satellites," where deserted or runaway young boys can be safe.

Neither of these two is content with school, though it is obvious that their intelligence is not the problem. They hide out in the school basement where the janitor has painstakingly helped install a simulation of the solar system and a planet named for Junior.

Social and psychological dynamics are prevalent as the author reveals, in layers, details about Junior; his mother, who has violent asthma attacks; the eccentric piano teacher; and Junior's secret drawings—all ingredients in his eventual mental breakdown. It is Buddy, hero of the streets, who takes Junior to one of his satellites with the assistance of the janitor. Here, the reader is left to assume, Junior will heal and not be caught up in mental institutions and a social system that have few clues and answers to the problems of such children, especially those whose lives are complicated by the negatives applied to Africanness in this society.

Few personal descriptors are used in the text here except in the case of the piano teacher: "her skin was light brown with a yellowish tint." Her mental strangeness is indicated by descriptions such as "she powdered her feet so she could follow her footprints and know when someone crossed her path"(42). At one point Junior Brown is described: "He looked like a giant, black Buddha" (3).

(M) *The Tombs of Atuan* by Ursula K. Le Guin. Atheneum.

This is book II of the Earthsea Trilogy. On the island of Atuan, a Kargish child is taken from her family and designated high priestess. As tradition dictates, the girl, Ahe, is renamed, consecrated to the gods, and dedicated to the service of the "Nameless Ones."

While she is allowed some time to play, Ahe's life is spent learning rituals and the layout of an underground labyrinth where the tombs of the Nameless Ones are found. Becoming fascinated with the places underground, Ahe memorizes the path of the labyrinth so that she can travel in the dark without being lost.

Later, Ahe finds the Wizard of Ged lost in the labyrinth and nearly dead. She saves him, not knowing how he should be punished. After learning more about Ged, the new priestess is convinced that she must help the man. With a stolen magic amulet, holding many powers, the two of them escape.

References are made to persons of color. Ahe asks her caretaker, Kossil, "'What do the wizard folk look like, are they truly black all over, with white eyes?'" Kossil answers, "'They are black and vile. I have never seen one'" (62). Ahe's description of the man she has captured in the labyrinth is "'His skin is dark, perhaps from the Inner Lands'" (80).

1974

Newbery Award

***The Slave Dancer* by Paula Fox. Bradbury.**
The horrors of the slave capturing and transporting system are chronicled in this book about a young boy, designated as *Creole*, who was shanghaied and forced to work as the *slave dancer* on a ship. To keep the captives' limbs from atrophying and generally to keep them alive for later sale, a process of bringing shackled slaves onto deck was employed. The victims were forced to move or dance while the boy played his fife.

The scene travels from New Orleans to the African coast and back to New Orleans, when the boy is able to escape his plight accompanied by a young male captive named Ras.

Many objections appeared in the book review literature concerning this title. Some regarded the author's constant use of "niggerisms" throughout the book and her initial blaming of Africans themselves for assisting in the capture of slaves. (See pages 23–24.) Also, there were objections to one African tribe being selected for reference as unsuitable for slaving. The captain states, "'I won't have Ibos. They're soft as melons and kill themselves if they are not watched twenty-four hours a day. I will not put up with some creatures'" (21). African chiefs holding slaves for sale to traders are mentioned. The boy is being told about the barracoon, which the British have set on fire: "'They've set the barracoon on fire, and the damned niggers that they [the chiefs] have held for us have run off and escaped! . . . That's the place where the chiefs keep them chained and ready to trade'" (52).

In some cases attempts are made to translate the boy's feelings: "'Now that I could gaze without restraint at the helpless and revealed forms of these slaves, was a mortification beyond any I had ever imagined.'" He faces many horrors, sickness, slaves getting sick and being thrown overboard, slaves being beaten and shot, and more, until he grows to hate the slaves; in a long passage, he details his hate (79). Why hate the slaves and not their captors?

In the end, an unlikely escape and return to the southern coast is contrived. The boy's life and that of the African slave boy, Ras, are saved by an old African American man named Daniel, a runaway slave himself.

The problems found with this story may originate with its being told from the point of view of a boy who lacks knowledge or concern about slavery. The slavers themselves obviously have no sympathy for the slaves. Meager attempts within the story to speak for the slaves fall flat. The horrors are certainly amplified, but humanity is lost as slaves become only a commodity.

1975

Newbery Award

+++*M. C. Higgins the Great* by Virginia Hamilton. Macmillan.

Mayo Cornelius Higgins, whose favorite place to sit is at the top of a flagpole, meets two new people who could change his life. The family lives on a fictional mountain in West Virginia, near the Ohio River, called Sarah's Mountain. Mayo is frustrated that his father does not seem to realize the slag-heap from strip mining at the back of his house is one day going to slide down and destroy the house. More than anything, M. C. wants to move from this place. When a stranger appears and speaks to him about his mother's singing, Mayo immediately has fantasies of a record contract and a move from the mountains.

The other person who enters Mayo's life is a young female traveler to whom he tells his story and shares his frustrations with his father. She provides him with words of wisdom, which help when he learns that there will be no recording contract and life must go on much the same.

The author uses no dialect but incorporates some of the colloquial vernacular; "There's where the dude come from," M. C. says, speaking of the visitor seeking music.

There are occasional physical descriptors: "M. C. was tall, with oak brown skin, like his mother. . . . He had hard strength and grace" (4). There are many descriptions of the place that give the reader a sense of being there. The author uses her masterful skills to weave a compelling story in an unusual place.

Honor Award

Figgs & Phantoms **by Ellen Raskin. Dutton.**
This is a very strange story about a family of little people, apparently an accepted part of the local town. It is Mona Lisa Figg Newton who becomes the lead in the story. She is ashamed of her "ex circus freaks" family but loves Uncle Florence. Together the two of them steal rare books from the local bookstore. Uncle Florence deals in rare books, and other members of the family are equally colorful, including an aunt who tap-dances incessantly.

After her uncle Florence dies, Mona attempts to search for him because he has always told her that at his death, he would go to the Isle of Capri. She spends a lot of time researching a way to join her uncle on the Isle.

For the purposes here, the notable passage is one when Mona is searching the library for information and tells the librarian "'I want *Children of the Sea* or *Nigger* . . .'" The words are out when Mona realizes that the librarian Miss Quigley, who has been her friend, storyteller, and helper with reference, is Black: "Rebecca Quigley's face froze in pained shock, Mona grabbed the book of Spanish maps from her hand and fled from the library sobbing." A title necessary to her search is *The Nigger of the Narcissus*. Mona is remorseful and continues to cry when she gets home but there is no follow-up, no apology or explanation.

(M) *My Brother Sam Is Dead* **by James Lincoln Collier and Christopher Collier. Four Winds.**
Timothy lives in Feading Ridge, Connecticut, during the Revolutionary War. His brother, Sam, serves in the revolutionary forces, while his father is a Loyalist. Arguments between Sam and his father drive Sam away.

Sam returns home only once to see his girlfriend and to visit his family. Later a cow is stolen from Sam's own family and members of the regiment frame Sam, who is innocent, for the theft. After sentencing, Sam is executed for the crime, while the distraught and despairing Timothy looks on.

There are no real images of African Americans here. An occasional slave is mentioned (144). At one point, Timothy's mother says, "You'll need somebody bigger than Jerry. Perhaps you can hire Sam Smith's Negro Ned'" (133).

+++*Philip Hall Likes Me, I Reckon Maybe* by Bette Greene. Dial.

Eleven-year-old Beth Lambert lives in Pocahontas, Arkansas. She is always second best in her class behind Philip Hall, the cutest and smartest boy in class. Although she is enamored of Philip, Beth is very smart and strives to go to college and become a veterinarian. She is unaware of her tendency to allow Philip to excel so that he will like her.

After several episodic events, including learning that she is allergic to dogs, Beth competes at the county fair and wins a blue ribbon for calf-raising, hoping her win will not anger Philip.

The colloquial language in this warm family story is smooth and easy. Descriptors are few but the overall picture is good. This is the first in a series of books about this character.

1976

Honor Award

+++*The Hundred Penny Box* by Sharon Bell Mathis. Illus. by Leo and Diane Dillon. Viking.

This a deeply sensitive story about a very young boy and his great-great-aunt, Aunt Dew. He has a special relationship with Aunt Dew, who sometimes forgets his name and even if he is there. He is attached to Aunt Dew and the hundred penny box that his mother would like to burn. Those are Aunt Dew's years in the box and Michael wants to hide it from his mother. Aunt Dew declares that if anybody takes her box, they will take her too.

When Michael and Aunt Dew count the pennies, Michael learns about the family and life in the past because for Aunt Dew each year has a story. The Dillons' beautiful, sepia-colored illustrations add enormous charm to this engaging story.

1977

Newbery Award

+++*Roll of Thunder, Hear My Cry* by Mildred D. Taylor. Dial.

An African American family faces racism in the South during the Depression. The story presents a positive picture of a warm family and of a strong father determined to protect and keep his land. The Logan family are presented as being both realistic and heroic. The word "nigger" is used only in the mouth of white racists: "'We want that thieving, murdering nigger of y'all's'" (251).

Physical descriptors are few, but the author manages to give her characters presence, which adds to their humanity.

1979

Newbery Award

+++*The Westing Game* by Ellen Raskin. Dutton.

One of the main characters in this story is "a tall black woman in a tailored suit." J. J. Ford, the first woman in the state to be elected to a judgeship, is one among an array of characters of various ethnicities. All are gathered to hear the will of Mr. Westing, whom some believe was murdered. Everyone is astounded when the will reads, "Today I have gathered together my nearest and dearest, my sixteen nieces and nephews."

As this mystery evolves and all the characters are delineated, each hopes to inherit some of Westing's fortunes.

It is the young girl called Turtle who eventually unravels all the complicated leads that have left others, including the judge, befuddled. Readers are enlightened with pieces of information. Judge Josie Jo Ford, for example, explains that she lived in the Westing household, where her mother was a servant. Her father worked on the railroad but was a gardener at the house on his days off. She describes herself as "the skinny, long legged black daughter of the servants" (148). The judge speaks of having spent her lonely moments playing chess with and being constantly beaten by Sam Westing. The last words he ever said to her were, "'Stupid child, you can't have a brain in that frizzy head to make a move like that'" (149). Westing paid for Ford to attend boarding school and go to college. She is unaware of other points at which he might have intervened in her life.

The African American character of the female judge is clearly delineated, with few of the negatives often applied to such characters. At one point, another fortune seeker thinks about the judge, "Unless she's one of those Black Panthers in disguise" (114). This insertion was added just for "color" and has no importance to the story.

Physical descriptions are few. One of the characters is Greek and in one passage the judge stares at his hand, which was "deep bronze": "She lowered her hands to her lap. His Greek skin was darker than her 'black' skin" (31).

The ending is a surprise for the readers, but it is noted that Judge Ford has been appointed to the United States Supreme Court. This is an entertaining mystery story, though somewhat complicated. This is one of the best of the multicultural stories this award offers.

Honor Award

+++*The Great Gilly Hopkins* by Katherine Paterson. Crowell.

Seven-year-old Gilly Hopkins is a tough young girl, lonely and frustrated after having moved from foster home to foster home. She longs for permanence but immediately puts up barriers when placed in her most recent home with an obese mother and a small boy. Nearby there lives an old blind Black man, Mr. Randolph.

When sent to his house with a dinner invitation, Gilly thinks she has the wrong house because she is not accustomed to socializing with people of another color. "I never touched one of those people in my life," she says (11).

As the story evolves, Gilly grows to love her family and wishes to stay with them even though earlier she had devised a plot to run away. She steals money from the blind neighbor but later regrets it. It is clear that Gilly's prejudices against people of color are due to ignorance. The author's psychology is apparent, but I am not sure young children will completely understand that Gilly's emotional condition leads to some of her troubles at home and at school. At school, she feels compelled to confront the African American teacher, Miss Harris. She cuts out a picture of an African American woman, "a tall, beautiful black woman in an Afro. Her skin was a little darker than Miss Harris' but it was close enough." She places the picture where the teacher can find it with an added note, "They're saying, 'Black is beautiful,' but . . . looks mighty like a person with a vested interest in maintaining this point of view."

This is not a heavy story; in fact, there are several light and humorous moments, including the night when Gilly's grandmother comes to visit. Mr. Randolph is sick and staying with Gilly and her family temporarily. The foster mother and brother also are sick with flu. Grandmother enters to find Mr. Randolph in his pajamas and the foster mother who collapses from weakness. Of course, the visiting woman doesn't know what to make of this scene.

Hoping one day to return, Gilly is taken away by the grandmother. Knowing what is best, her foster mother encourages her to stay with her natural family.

1980

Newbery Award

+++A Gathering of Days: A New England Girl's Journal, 1830–1832 by Joan W. Blos. Scribner.

A nineteen-year-old girl named Catherine is the journal writer and the heroine of the story. Set in the pre–Civil War period, the narrative follows Catherine's life as a surrogate mother to her young sister, Matty. Their mother died in childbirth. Cassie Shipman is Catherine's best friend, who dies of fever further on in the story. Asa Shipman, Cassie's brother, is also a major character.

The story is designed to sympathize with a young woman showing great courage in sadness. It also deals with those who are stereotyped by the community and with a runaway slave discovered by Asa Shipman and Catherine. Together, the two find ways to help the slave. After his departure Catherine wonders if his escape was successful. She is shown as innocent and having little knowledge of slavery: "'A negro, Asa? We've had none before, neither slave or free. So I couldn't know what it might mean to call him dark complected.'" She speaks of having read from Garrison's writings about slavery, noting a bill of sale: "A black girl, 17 years of age of excellent character, and of good disposition; a very useful and handy person in a house for a turn of years." After reading, Catherine wonders, "Would not a black girl know love and fear?" (46). Several passages follow in which the main character wonders about people of color, slave and free. She mentions the famous abolitionist newspaper *The Liberator* and quotes from it.

Others confront issues of the times. In arguments between the teacher and Catherine's father, her father asks, "'But would you want then . . . to have a black man as your neighbor?'" (45). Discussion of the movement for the establishment of a Negro nation in Liberia, with which her father agrees, is also inserted (120).

Eventually, Catherine receives a message from the man she and Asa had helped escape, and he is indeed free. In a package, he has sent crocheted lace and a message, "Sisters Bless You, Free Now, Curtis in Canada."

There are other events in the story that concern Catherine, including her father's remarriage. Somehow the format is depersonalizing so that it is hard to closely identify with characters in an overall good story.

1983

Newbery Award

+++*Dicey's Song* by Cynthia Voigt. Atheneum.
This is the second in a series of books about the Tillerman family, Dicey, James, Maybeth, and Sammy. When their mother experiences an emotional breakdown and leaves the children, Dicey decides to take the family from Provincetown, Massachusetts, to Crisfeld, Maryland, hoping to live with their grandmother. Their travels are not easy because the children have little money, but they manage to make the trip. Upon arriving, the children find a grandparent who is a reclusive oddball and not too welcoming. As time passes, their grandmother begins to relate more positively to the children.

Thirteen-year-old Dicey faces the usual aspects of adolescent questioning and self-examination but added to this is her role of surrogate parent to her siblings. She finds it hard to give up this role and allow her grandmother to lead the family. In addition, each individual child has problems, including Maybeth, who is mentally challenged.

Facing this extraordinary set of problems, Dicey finds school boring, but she eventually makes friends with Wilhemina, who is the only prominent African American character in the book. Wilhemina makes the first overture, asking Dicey to be her partner in a science assignment. After introductions, the Black girl is described: "She smiled at Dicey, and her teeth flashed white and her round cheeks got rounder. Her skin was smooth and milk-chocolate brown. Her hands . . . were large and quick." Wilhemina is further portrayed as quite self-assured, saying about herself, "'I mean, I'm pretty smart, and certainly smarter than most of the kids around here, I'm black. I'm a black female. Oh and—well look at me. Tell the truth, I could be thirty years old and have kids of my own, couldn't I? Big as I am. If you just look. See what I mean?'" Wilhemina details her reasons for wanting to pursue a friendship with Dicey, describing herself more as a "'giant oddball . . . with more personality than anybody needs.'" Dicey begins to accept "Mina" as a friend and confidant.

The images here are mixed, and questions that must be asked are: Why is it that an African American friend is often portrayed as a big person? Do characters have to be oddballs in order to justify a relationship between a person of color and a white girl?

Honor Award

+++*Sweet Whispers, Brother Rush* by Virginia Hamilton. Philomel.

Hamilton did not shy away from offering her readers complexity and mystery. A young girl named Tree, struggling with her life and surroundings, sees a ghost, Brother Rush. At first, she assumes that Brother Rush is a real person: "It was like the figure of him jumped right out of space at her" (10). Brother Rush is described as having "skin that was a pale brown with a good sprinkling of reddish freckles. He had refined features and full lips. His large nose was long, straight, with flared nostrils. His hair had the same reddish tint of the freckles, soft and tightly curled."

Tree lives in an apartment with her brother, Dab, who has special needs. He has always had headaches and other strange symptoms. Her mother works away from home and comes when she can with money and food for her two children. Vy, her mother, "had deep dimples . . . the kind they sang songs about."

Later, Tree learns that while she is struggling alone, her mother has developed another life and relationships while away from home, including having a male friend and a car.

One day, Tree finds Dab has become really sick, too sick to ignore, so she calls her mother. Vy comes home, bringing the boyfriend with her. More physical descriptors are offered: "He was darker in color than M'Vy. There was a red hue to his dark skin. . . . Like somebody re-color some chocolate" (125). This is followed by a full paragraph of descriptors other authors shy away from or simple don't have the skills to supply.

Meanwhile, Tree still sees the ghost of Brother Rush and is having visions that take her back to her mother's earlier life. Through these encounters she learns a few things that cause her to confess her visits with the ghost and allows her mother the opportunity to fill in gaps about the past.

When Dab becomes hospitalized and dies, Tree is distraught, but her mother finds a satisfactory answer to their living situation and life begins to look more positive. The author, again, presents us with outstanding writing and unforgettable images.

1984

Honor Award

+++*A Solitary Blue* **by Cynthia Voight. Atheneum.**

Jeff Greene is the "solitary" blue. His life is complicated by the fact that his mother has left and his father is distant and attempting to be unemotional. Jeff decides to do everything he can to please his father—cooking, cleaning, and so forth. The two maintain a formal, almost cold relationship, but Jeff manages to survive.

After a time, Jeff's mother contacts them and asks if Jeff can come to visit her in South Carolina. Jeff becomes immediately enamored with his mother and the life she lives with his grandmother in a big house. Questions about the veracity of his mother's comments, male relationships, and so on, lie beneath the surface. On his second visit, he learns that his mother is a liar and that many of the things she told him about loving him and wanting to be with him are untrue. In fact, the mother is a spoiled, self-centered woman, prone to dependent relationships with men.

Jeff loses his sense of balance and begins to fail in school. With the help of a friend, his father makes an effort to find solutions. Finally they move. In the new place, Jeff meets the Tillermans of the author's previous book, *Dicey's Song*. Because he is entranced with the Tillermans and falls in love with Dicey, Jeff comes out of his solitary shell.

There are intermittent glimpses of African Americans through Miss Opal, who works for his grandmother. When Jeff visits Charleston, she praises him for his personal neatness and tells him stories about the Black community locally and on the nearby islands

(55–56). Miss Opal's son Willum is in jail. There is also a man whom Jeff meets at the wharf. He questions the man about getting a boat (107). Jeff asks "the nameless black man" about rowing, river currents, and more before buying a boat (109). The boat provides transportation for Jeff to visit one of the islands. He has heard about these places where Black people live from Miss Opal (115).

The man with the boat speaks very little local dialect, such as "suh" and "Whuffo" (what for) (107). Miss Opal speaks none.

1985

Honor Award

The Moves Make the Man by Bruce Brooks. Harper.

A complex story is told in first person by Jerome, who practices basketball in a dark, secret place in the woods. Basketball is used as a metaphor for life. Complexities begin when Jerome is the first African American sent to integrate the Chestnut Street Junior High School. There, he tries out for the basketball team but is not allowed to play because he is African American.

At the new school Bix Braxton Rivers, who asks Jerome to teach him how to play hoops, enters the story. Bix is a strange young man, with his own tragic problems. Jerome likes Bix and takes him to his secret place to practice. When Jerome wins a railroad lantern in a game, they have light. Jerome wants to teach Bix fakes, the moves that he uses to win. Bix refuses to learn fakes, which he considers the same as lies and trickery. Soon, Bix's conflict with his stepfather is revealed and he tells Jerome why he has to beat his stepfather at playing hoops.

All of this is followed by the later scenes of Bix's visit to see his mother in a mental hospital. These scenes are sad, gripping, and tragic.

There are some questionable passages, which may not be absolutely necessary to add to the reality of the book. They are probably the author's attempts to show how victims often co-opt the derogatory terms used against them. Sometimes the use of such terms reveals an underlying anger. In one case, Jerome is thinking about the move to Chestnut Street School: "They had to start letting *jiga-boo* boys and girls into their schools. Nobody ever thought to make the *jigaboos* let little crackers into their schools" (49). "I guess my situation was ripe for trouble, being the only *coon* in the forest, like one of my uncles said" (56).

Although the reference to "Nigger! calls" from some students (57) is probably real, in the interjection of Jerome's friendship with James Knox Polk Peters, there are comments about James's daddy saying to his son, "'You get your young black butt in here right now where I can beat it blue!'" (40). This quote is certainly not beyond reality, but what's the point? Polk also refers to Jerome as "nigger" (40).

Why does the author have Jerome go on for one long paragraph describing a white woman, her face and hair, and all the black people who are aware of her beauty, while in one line he says, "I think my momma is pretty and stronger looking than any other person, but this white woman just knocked you in the eye"? It later becomes evident that this view of the woman is probably meant to compare with the later view of Bix's crazed mother, but will young people get it?

There is a passage in which Jerome learns the power of words and that one can define himself by learning to use the right words (60).

1986

Honor Award

Commodore Perry in the Land of the Shogun by Rhoda Blumberg. Lothrop.

The story of Perry's attempts to open relationships and trade with the Japanese is illustrated with black-and-white drawings. Images of African Americans appear in the very beginning when Perry is pictured as arriving in full uniform, even though it is July and the weather is hot: "When he landed, Perry was flanked by two tall handsome black bodyguards, who proved to be sensational. The Japanese had never seen black men before."

After his first visit, Perry returned in the spring with a larger fleet as he had promised the Japanese. Perry had insisted that his men be rewarded with entertainment. The men aboard the ship *Powhatan* were entertained by the Ethiopian minstrels. The author explains in parenthesis: "(Minstrel shows were the rage in pre–Civil War America, in both the slave states and in the North. Entertainers blackened their faces in order to caricature poor, uneducated blacks. There were skits, jokes, and song-and-dance routines.)" The minstrels also entertained the Japanese. The comment made was, "They were amused by the blackened faces, banjos, tambourines and silly dancing. . . . They knew nothing about Africans who had been brought to America as slaves." Blackfaced dancers are illustrated.

1988

Newbery Award

Lincoln: A Photobiography by Russell Freedman. Clarion.
This author has a knack for choosing a set of photographs around which a biography can be formed. This is good history presented in a fashion that may lead readers to further study.

Lincoln is studied here as a real person, not a cardboard hero. The author gives insight to conflicting opinions about the man. The issues of slavery of course are a major part of the story.

Honor Book

(M) *After the Rain* by Norma Fox Mazer. Morrow.
Rachel is troubled by her appearance and her lack of friends. Her parents are older and are somewhat unaware of their child's insecurities. In addition, there is grandfather Izzy, a rather cantankerous old guy. Rachel has not been very close to her grandfather, until his health begins to fail. Her mother is worried but does not have time to spend with her father, since she works daily.

The young girl begins daily walks and visits with Izzy. She slowly learns to love him, and he reluctantly returns her affection. Rachel for the first time hears about her grandfather's work on local bridges and that Izzy placed his handprint in the cement of one bridge. When Izzy dies, Rachel and a newly found friend, Lewis, search for the handprint on all the local bridges. After many searches, the handprint is found, from which Rachel makes a paper print. She also realizes that a part of her grandfather will remain with her forever.

There are no African American characters in this book, but there is one paragraph that makes it worthy of inclusion here. Early in the story it is noted, "Every Thursday night Rachel watches *The Cosby Show* with amazement in her heart. Look at that wise, funny daddy! Look at those gorgeous sisters and cute hunk of a brother." The sad fact is that there is no evidence of this very positive appreciation in her life, at school, or at home.

1989

Honor Award

+++*In the Beginning: Creation Stories from Around the World* by Virginia Hamilton. Harcourt.

The author presents a group of creation stories including Olurun the Creator from the Yoruba, Nyambi the Creator from Zambia, Mawu-Lisa the Creators from the Abomey people, Republic of Benin, and more.

+++*Scorpions* by Walter Dean Myers. Harper.

Myers writes with knowledge and insight about life in the city, especially those on the lower rungs of society. He presents a poignant family story with elements of the complex necessities of everyday life. Relationships, male struggles in society, the meaning of friendship, and more are all part of this narrative.

Jamal, his sister Sassy, and their single-parent mother live a life of basic survival, with small joys. Randy, their older brother, goes to jail, leaving everyone saddened and disturbed. Life becomes even more complicated when Jamal visits Randy in jail. Randy speaks to him about the possibilities of being released, if he can get five hundred dollars to appeal his case.

Jamal seeks work and considers going to the Scorpions, a local gang, to get the money. He is hesitant about being involved with the gang and confides in his best friend, Tito, a Puerto Rican boy. Jamal does make the contact after having little success finding and keeping a job. The eventual contacts and involvement with the Scorpions lead to trouble for Jamal. Because of his commitment to friendship, Tito faces undeserved troubles.

The author offers the reader descriptors like "Sassy was eight, and coffee colored like her father" and "mama was dark like he was" (9).

1991

Newbery Award

+++*Maniac Magee* by Jerry Spinelli. Little, Brown.
Issues regarding segregated communities, myths about people who are different, and the breaking down of those barriers are covered in an amazingly well-written story about a homeless orphan, Maniac Magee. Maniac becomes a legend and a hero until, at last, he finds a home where he experiences love and family like he has never known. But happiness is thwarted because Maniac, who is Caucasian, has become part of an African American family. There are negative community reactions.

Intricately, the author weaves a tale of love, family, and positive relationships lost and regained, without the projection of stereotypes. Although Maniac is the protagonist and an engaging hero, one of the leaders of the African American gang finds himself in a most unusual situation and emerges as equally heroic. With verve, humor, and compassion, the story exudes love! Indeed, this book is a celebration of life.

Honor Award

+++*The True Confessions of Charlotte Doyle* by Avi. Jackson/Orchard.

Thirteen-year-old Charlotte Doyle describes her voyage in 1892 aboard the *Seahawk*. For various reasons, she is the only female aboard ship. She is befriended by the old Black cook named Zachariah, whom she meets again after returning safely to her family. There is mystery, suspense, and a vivid view of sailing portrayed, though Charlotte's situation is unusual.

Zachariah not only befriends Charlotte but also gives her a knife for protection. She rejects his friendship and tries to form an alliance with the unsavory captain. This leads to the story's nearly tragic events.

Although descriptions of Zachariah portray him as haggard, wrinkled, and frightening, this portrayal does not appear offensive but designed to emphasize the man's hard life. Zachariah seems central to the plot, but it is interesting to read many reviews that never recognize his presence in the story.

1993

Honor Award

+++*The Dark-Thirty: Southern Tales of the Supernatural* by Patricia C. McKissack. Illus. by Brian Pinkney. Knopf.

Historical notes introduce each of these tales. "Dark-thirty," according to author, is the half hour just before nightfall and the darkness. These original tales include themes of slavery, the Ku Klux Klan, conjure women, and root doctors. All are familiar themes in southern African American lore. The flavor of these stories reveals strong African connections with appropriate illustrations.

+++*Somewhere in the Darkness* by Walter Dean Myers. Scholastic.

Jimmy, the protagonist, has lived in the protective, disciplined, and loving care of Mama Jean and is surviving in a tough tenement neighborhood when his father, "Crab," surprisingly appears. Crab has been in jail and now plans to take his son on a trip. What seems to be a simple matter of a father trying to create a new life for himself and his alienated son evolves as a disturbing story of a father's desperation and attempt at redemption. The ending is tragic. Positive relationships between Jimmy, Mama Jean, and tenement neighbors counter the negative forces of a father unable to remove himself from what has become a way of life. Intense passages amplify confrontations between father and son.

Early in the story, creative descriptors are offered: "The mahogany framing the oval glass was nearly the same color as his face." Social symbolism is obvious in a later description of a small girl in Arkansas, where Jimmy's father has taken him. She is described with dark skin and a fat stomach and carrying a blond doll.

1995

Honor Award

+++*The Ear, the Eye, and the Arm* by Nancy Farmer. Jackson/Orchard.

A futuristic story of myth and lore set in Zimbabwe in the year 2194. The author provides a glossary of terms from the Shona people of Zimbabwe, who are the main inhabitants of the story. Love for Zimbabwe is reflected in the author's tone, including many pleas for cultural survival, environmental watchfulness, and human understanding amid some trickery and humor. This is a most interesting fantasy and mystery. Helping the three children in the story solve the mystery are Ear—superhearing, Eye—supersight, and Arm—long limbs.

1996

Honor Award

++++*The Watsons Go to Birmingham—1963* by Christopher Paul Curtis. Delacorte.

This is a wonderful African American story that in the beginning appears to be focused on the angst of the teenage boy in the family. In fact, it is his actions that cause the Watsons to make a car trip to Birmingham. The main characters are Mom, Dad, sister Joetta, and brother Byron, and the story is told through the eyes of ten-year-old Kenny.

The car trip exposes some of the problems faced by African Americans during segregation. For example, everyone wonders if the father will survive driving so many miles without sleep simply because accommodations for them are few, if any. After the family arrives in Birmingham, the central incident of the story occurs. Witnessed is the historical bombing of the church in which four young African American girls died. Readers are drawn into the incident because Joetta, who is at the church, is lost in the resulting turmoil. Kenny fears that she is one of the dead.

The Watson family survives the tragic event while the young people are forced to grow up in a terrible way. All of this is balanced by the characterizations, which are sometimes very humorous, especially that of the father. This is not a historical document but an enjoyable family story with strong reminders of the plight of African Americans during this period.

+++*Yolanda's Genius* by Carol Fenner. Margaret McElderry/ Simon & Schuster.

Yolanda is a big girl for her age—bigger than any of the other children in her fifth-grade class—and she is taunted because of it. She is responsible for the care of her younger brother, who is in first grade. His name is Andrew, and his constant companion is a mouth harp, which he has taught himself to play.

To escape the dangers of dope and other problems of the city, Yolanda's mother moves the family from Chicago to a small town nearby. Her husband having died, she is a single parent and seeks the best for her two children.

At the new school, Yolanda forms a friendship with a Caucasian girl, an outcast. The fact that the only Caucasian girl who befriends Yolanda is an outcast is problematic, but it seems the author assumes society would rule this portrayal as the most realistic.

Yolanda is the first to recognize that her brother, Andrew, is a musical genius and determines to get him help and recognition.

She is portrayed as thoughtful and aggressive, so the somewhat unlikely ending at a jazz festival in Chicago seems possible. The story is one of family and caring between brother and sister in the midst of the usual school difficulties of bullies and more. Yolanda is presented without any hesitation as being smart. She makes good grades and seems to have no problems of self-esteem in spite of being bigger. This has been called a "Cinderella" story and it is, but it is worth reading.

1997

Honor Award

+++*A Girl Named Disaster* by Nancy Farmer. Richard Jackson/Orchard Books.

With directions from her grandmother, Nhamo escapes an arranged marriage by boat. She hopes to find her father's family in Zimbabwe. Her heroic journey is fraught with danger, an encounter with a colony of baboons, dangers on the river, hunger, and mythological African spirits. The journey is compelling reading with traditional African stories interspersed throughout.

Nhamo and others are referred to as "beautiful," though few other descriptors are used. The author reveals knowledge of and respect for African culture. Appended are a glossary, informational notes, and a bibliography.

1999

Newbery Award

++++*Holes* by Louis Sachar. Frances Foster.

The main character, Stanley Yelnats, is sent to a youth correction camp. He is one of a group of seven—three Caucasians, three Blacks, and one Hispanic. As described in the book, "Stanley was thankful that there were no racial problems. X-Ray, Armpit, and Zero were black. He, Squid, and Zigzag were white. Magnet was

Hispanic. On the lake they were all the same reddish color—color of dirt." None of the characters except "Zigzag" are described in physical detail. The author concentrates more on revealing the psychological and family problems related to their incarceration. Even Stanley is not described physically, except we know he is big and is of Latvian descent.

Two of the African American characters figure strongly in the story. The author presents X-Ray as a leader of the group and Zero as quietly strange. Unlike the others, Zero loves to dig. Each day, the boys spend hours in the sun digging holes with precise dimensions, and they are directed to present any unusual findings to the warden. For complex reasons, Zero escapes the camp followed by Stanley, dubbed "Caveman." Although called "Zero," this character emerges as heroic in the end, becoming the partner and friend of the main character, Stanley Yelnats.

Added to the fact that this is an unusual, intricately woven story for young people, the African American characters are far from stereotyped. Even though Zero can't read, he is extremely astute at math. The African Americans are not the main characters, but they emerge strongly.

2000

Newbery Award

+++Bud, Not Buddy by Christopher Paul Curtis. Delacorte.

Bud's saga begins in Flint, Michigan, in 1936, when times are hard following the Great Depression. Hordes of the poor of all ethnic groups live in shantytowns and travel on the rails seeking a better life. Bud has lived in and been brutalized by foster families. He runs away to search for his father. Items in his battered suitcase were given to him by his mother. With these items, he expects to identify the man he thinks is his father. After some misadventures, Bud finds a small group of traveling Black musicians based in Grand Rapids and led by the man he is seeking.

There is no immediate reconciliation between Bud and his possible father. The female singer with the group intervenes, protecting and caring for Bud. The story evolves into a mystery about Bud's real identity with a surprising but satisfying ending. In the conclusion, he discovers a new family and learns to love the music called jazz. He has his own instrument and vows to become a member of the group.

There are no heavy stereotypes in the character portrayals or the language, though some of the language of musicians is rightfully used. The reader learns a bit about the life of a foster child, the difficulties of those caught up in the Great Depression, and mostly about the importance of family, whether formed by bloodlines or just by love.

2001

Honor Award

+++*Hope Was Here* by Joan Bauer. G. P. Putnam's Sons.

"Tulip" officially changes her name to Hope. She lives with her aunt, the substitute mother who nurtures her, while her biological mother visits once in a while. Tulip and Aunt move around a lot because their business is food service and the jobs are not lasting. Aunt cooks and Hope is a waitress, as is her biological mom. The story is a tribute to diners, cooks, and waitresses committed to their work because they care about people. A diner is the setting for most of the story.

Uniquely exposed are the intricacies, complications, and ruthlessness found in politics as G. T., owner of the diner, runs for election for mayor of his town. Corruption and trickery abound.

In one of the few stories in which African American characters are an integral part of the community, a friendship actually exists between the white diner owner and the African American minister. Also, one positively portrayed character is an African American head waitress in the diner. Hope describes Flo, the head waitress, as follows: "She had a beautiful face and short full hair. I liked her smile."

An interesting view of life surrounded by food and food service is offered. In addition, this is a poignant story about love and family that sadly ends with the death of G. T., the diner owner. By the time of his death, he is Hope's new father. But in the end, she has shared two years of love with him and Aunt during his period of remission from leukemia.

2002

Honor Award

+++Carver: A Life in Poems by Marilyn Nelson. Front Street.
Details about the life of George Washington Carver are presented in poems. His adoption by a white family, his leaving to find education, and his accomplishments at the Tuskegee Institute are woven into verse. Illustrations include some historical notes and photographs.

2004

Honor Award

+++An American Plague: The True and Terrifying Story of the Yellow Fever Epidemic of 1793 by Jim Murphy. Clarion Books.
A factual, documented narrative about the yellow fever epidemic that struck Philadelphia in 1793 is a rare offering. The new nation's seat of government was decimated by fear and death. Information about the causes of the epidemic is carefully detailed along with medical practices of the time. There were no miracle drugs, but by today's standards, rather primitive curative methods were used.

While many vacated the city, the Free African Society stepped forward as heroes and set up cadres of nurses and caretakers for the sick. It was believed that people of African descent were immune to the fever, but this was not true. Some persons *had* developed anti-bodies to the fever because they had lived in places where malaria and other similar diseases had been prevalent. Many African Americans became sick and died during the epidemic, but those who could continued working diligently to save the sick. The little-known facts about these events and the attempts following the epidemic to vilify African Americans are presented factually and fairly as part of the complete historical picture of this disastrous period in America's history. Competitive practices among doctors in gaining fame are noted along with the resulting methods of mosquito control.

2005

Honor Award

+++*Lizzie Bright and the Buckminster Boy* by Gary D. Schmidt. Clarion Books/Houghton Mifflin.
 Although Lizzie becomes the main focus, this is Turner Buck-minster's story. Turner and his family move to Phippsburg, Maine, where his father, a minister, heads a new church. Turner discovers Lizzie, an African American girl, who lives on the nearby Island of Malega in a community founded by former slaves. After meeting Lizzie, Turner's whole world changes. He admits never having met or having shaken the hand of a "negro" before. His growing admiration of Lizzie becomes apparent when Turner confronts the ban imposed on his trips to the Malega Island. There, he has become friends with Lizzie's grandfather and others. He loves everything about these people and does not understand the political rumblings that threaten to move residents off the island. The church and his father are culprits in the removal of the island's residents, though Turner's father later regrets his involvement. A poignant story evolves with dire results for Lizzie and her grandfather, while Turner takes heroic steps to save the young girl whom he has grown to love.
 The author deftly offers insight regarding the inner workings and tyranny of racism when combined with religion. It becomes obvious how effectively these tools can be used against innocent

people. Without preaching, but by the devices of the story, moral lessons are taught.

Schmidt uses poetic descriptors that imply Turner's growing affection for Lizzie: "And Turner watching the flow of her arms and hands, the fine long fingers that twirled the ball just before they released it, the eyes that in the clear air shone with the brightness of the day."

+++*The Voice That Challenged a Nation: Marian Anderson and the Struggle for Equal Rights* by Russell Freedman. Clarion Books/Houghton Mifflin.

Complete with numerous photographs of the singer in concert, of family, and of the famous singer in her historic appearance at the Lincoln Monument is this biography. When Marian Anderson was barred by the DAR from singing at Constitution Hall, protests arose. The involvement of Walter White of the NAACP and others emphasizes that the fight for civil rights did not begin in Alabama. The rudeness, embarrassment, indignity, and helplessness faced by the African American singer are explicit. Institutionalized racism in her own country is made more blatant by documentation of Ms. Anderson's warm acceptance in European countries. Offered here is the picture of a dignified, talented young woman who, against the odds, is determined to develop her talent and present it to the world. Enough details of career and family relationships are included in this slim volume to give it some personal flavor.

It is no surprise that the newspapers referred to Anderson as "handsome." In those days African American women were often described in this manner. The author, however, refers to Marian Anderson as follows: "Offstage, Marian's quiet beauty and unaffected charm had always attracted suitors."

2006

Honor Award

(M) *Hitler Youth: Growing Up in Hitler's Shadow* by Susan Campbell Bartoletti. Scholastic.

This title traces the lives of various young people and their involvement in the Hitler Youth, some willingly and others reluctantly. Hitler's propaganda and its effect on the youth are vividly exposed. Attitudes toward Blacks are mentioned only in the context of Germany's sponsorship of and involvement in the Olympics. The book is included here because there is one strong statement about Jesse Owens: "But Hitler's superior Aryan race theories were shattered by a young African American college student named Jesse Owens, who won an unprecedented four gold medals in track events." This fact is somewhat dismissed by touting the thirty-three gold medals in other categories won by Germany. The author, however, makes a bold statement about race in general, which probably would not have appeared in earlier books for children: "Today scientists agree that 'race' is a meaningless concept since human differences are only skin deep." The presentation is an important one because it is made readily apparent how propaganda and lies can manipulate people; and how blaming a people for the plight of a nation was orchestrated into the horrible tragedy of the Holocaust. Recognition is made clear that so-called good people will often rally with those in power or stand by and allow atrocities to happen.

+++*Show Way* by Jacqueline Woodson. Illus. by Hudson Talbott. G. P. Putnam's Sons.

Profusely and colorfully illustrated, this is the poetic story of an African American family's traditions of storytelling, sewing, and quilting. With each creation, girls and boys are taught that there is a "way" or a path to freedom. Women of four generations lovingly teach their offspring the lore and the skills.

2008

Honor Award

+++*Elijah of Buxton* by Christopher Paul Curtis. Scholastic.

Buxton is a town in Canada settled by African American escaped slaves. Elijah was born in that town and knows only what he has learned from adults about slavery. He is the town's first child born in freedom and maintains the nebulous honor of having vomited on Frederick Douglass when Elijah was a baby and the famous abolitionist visited their town. Through sometimes humorous and sometimes tragically poignant episodes and events, the story provides a picture of everyday life in this supportive African American community just across the border from Michigan.

Characters in the story reveal the pain and hopefulness among those who have arrived in this place and their concerns for the many who remain in captivity. Elijah, who is almost twelve, increasingly becomes aware of these sentiments. Gradually the plot begins to revolve around Mr. Leroy, who plans to purchase the freedom of his family, still slaves. His money is stolen by the thieving Reverend Zachariah. A complex series of events leads to Elijah's crossing the border into America, encountering a group of shackled slaves, and bringing the baby on horseback to Buxton.

In spite of some events that appear improbable, the story is compelling reading and will familiarize the reader with details of life, rituals, and so forth among freedmen in Canada. As we have observed in other titles, especially wartime stories, in unusual times children are called upon to accomplish unusual feats. Historical information that provided background for this story is noted by the author at the end.

+++*Feathers* by Jacqueline Woodson. G. P. Putnam's Sons.

Frannie struggles with the concept of hope as she becomes intrigued by the poem read in class by her teacher—"Hope is the Thing with Feathers." When a new boy arrives at school, the first white to attend, he is taunted by his classmates and dubbed "Jesus" because of the way he wears his hair. The taunting brings focus on the perpetrators, one of whom is Trevor, whose father is white and absent from the home. In this community, African Americans and Caucasians live in separate communities, on either side of the highway.

Meantime, Samantha, daughter of a preacher, suggests to her best friend Frannie that Jesus may be the real thing. More taunting occurs and a verbal confrontation between Trevor and Jesus reveals

Trevor's insecurities about the missing father, and it is learned that Jesus has been adopted by his African American family.

This is a slight episodic story, with strength in its confrontation of real issues. Racial identification, family, deafness, mixed parentage, bullying, and friendship are all ingredients in 118 pages. Images and characterizations are clear and positive. African American families are normal, facing commonly understood issues.

2009

Honor Award

+++ *After Tupac and D Foster* by Jacqueline Woodson. G. P. Putnam's Sons.

The title sounds like this is a book about music, but don't be misled; it is much, much more. It is a story about family, forming friendships and allegiances, about dreams, about society's views of race, Black men, and homosexuality. All of this is contained in a pleasing story about three girls in the city who become friends. The protagonist, "The Brain," tells us the story of herself, Neeka, and D Foster, who just happens by one day. D considers the music and events that surround Tupac as an allegory of her own life. She is a foster child who has been left alone by her mother and displaced from one foster home to another. Determined to make her present placement a permanent one, she tries to do everything right. She and the other two spend as much time as they can together, following at all times the career, arrests, incarcerations, and eventual death of Tupac. The story itself is a metaphor for many lives and alerts us to the roles that music, hip-hop, and adoration of stars play in the hopes and desires of many. All of today's young adults will find some things to which they can relate in this story.

The author is astute in her aesthetic descriptions, giving readers a positive view of the way secure African American girls see themselves. The characterization of Neeka's homosexual brother is one of the most insightful and loving ones I have read in a book for teens.

+++*The Surrender Tree: Poems of Cuba's Struggle for Freedom* by **Margarita Engle. Holt.**
Poetic voices of persons involved in Cuba's historic struggles for freedom from Spain place any willing readers amid the plight of the people. Rosa, Lieutenant Death, José, Lieutenant-General Valeriano Nicolau, Marquis of Tenerife, Empire of Spain, and Silvia are the characters who describe the events, methods, and tragedies of war and brief moments of peace in Cuba from 1850 to 1899. Captured by the text, the reader experiences the beauty and wonder of the countryside as Rosa collects herbs and flowers for healing and travels with her to "deep forest, in caves of sparkling crystal hidden under waterfalls" (4), where she uses her knowledge of healing to cure runaway slaves. In contrast, Lieutenant Death is a slavehunter who coldly speaks of the "little witch" whom he continually hunts down until the end of the book. He is the one who sits by the pile of ears cut from the slaves for punishment and returns runaways to their owners. His job continues even when slaves are declared free. We are briefly joyful about freedom but despair when war and conflict continue and we must escape from one hiding place to another. As did the peasants, we learn of the reconcentration camps, planned as a strategy to finally erase all remnants of protest, but they don't work. We wonder what gives Rosa and later her husband José the strength and resolve to continue their mission of healing. Silvia, who has learned of Rosa from her grandmother, joins the healing forces, avoiding being placed in the camps.

This is one of the most powerful statements about the futility of war that I have ever read. The slaves here are not docile or simple-minded, but they return time after time to the fight, determined to be free.

Reviews:
Ancillary Titles

THE FOLLOWING TITLES ARE NEWBERY AWARD WINNERS or honor books that have tangential references to Africans or African Americans and books about other minorities emphasizing elements of culture and prejudice.

1922

Honor Award

***The Golden Fleece and the Heroes Who Lived Before Achilles* by Padraic Colum. Illus. by Willy Pogany. Macmillan.**

These ancient myths contain no references to Africans, but when Theseus sets out to destroy the minotaur, "he arose and he saw a *dark-faced* servant, who beckoned to him." "Dark-faced" is an almost useless descriptor considering the many variations of darker populations in the world.

Colum presents a classic retelling of familiar stories from ancient myths. All are focused on the Argonauts' search for the golden fleece. Fans of these myths will recognize Jason of the Argonauts, the sorceress Medea, Hercules, and others.

1925

Newbery Award

Tales from Silver Lands **by Charles Finger. Doubleday.**
A collection of nineteen tales from the author's travels in Central and South America. These are traditional folktales with animals, witches, and magic. Some cultural references and descriptions of places are found, but these are mostly tales to be read aloud or told. Although recorded in the early twentieth century, these tales would reflect African cultural influences in these geographic areas.

1928

Honor Award

Downright Dency **by Caroline Snedeker. Doubleday.**
In seventeenth-century Nantucket, Dency (Dionis) lives in the higher circles on the island. She meets and determines to save young Sam Jetsam from his life with a drunken female caretaker. Sam is a half-breed and would be ignored by most. Together the two have many adventures and begin to truly care for each other.

This title has been reissued and may provide insights for modern readers to the rigid systems and prejudices practiced in New England during these times. Of special interest is early cultural rejection of Quakers, known for their participation in the escapes of many African American slaves.

1929

Honor Award

The Boy Who Was **by Grace Hallock. Dutton (out of print).**
Although there were not enough references to Africans to include this title in our "image" list, in one story about the escape of a wounded Goth from the Byzantines, there is a passage in which "they spat on the barbarians, the vandals of Africa, the fair-haired

English slave boys, the dark-skinned Saracens, the heretic Spaniards and the yellow-haired Lombards" (64).

An artist visiting in the mountains of coastal Italy in 1927 discovers Nino the goatherd and his carvings of famous Mediterranean
people. Nino tells stories about each person he has carved and in
every story Nino appears as a goat keeper. The tales include those
of Odysseus, Pompeii, and the Crusaders—all historical fantasies.
There are some religious references, such as a boy visited by the
Lord Jesus asking him to deliver a sepulchre from the Saracens.

1930

Honor Award

The Jumping-Off Place by Marian Hurd McNeely. Longmans (out of print).

In this title, as in many covering this historical period, one of
the books being read is *Uncle Tom's Cabin*, considered a classic of
the times. We can assume that many images of African Americans
were formed from the reading of that title.

A family of homesteaders move to the Dakota prairies, where
they face winds, drought, and heat in their attempt to survive. The
uniqueness of this piece is that four children make this adventur-
ous move alone. Two brothers and two sisters are left alone without
adult supervision when their Uncle Jim dies. He has been their
guardian since their parents died earlier.

Animosity and cooperation are constant factors in the lives
of the homesteading families. The Welps are the young peoples'
enemies, but support is found from other families nearby. The
older children take care of the younger ones and, in spite of many
obstacles, they survive.

Pran of Albania by Elizabeth C. Miller. Illus. by Maud and
Miska Petersham. Doubleday (out of print).

One of the early chapters of this book is titled "Man of the
Blackface," which is apparently symbolic of traitor or evil. A continuing problem in presenting positive representation of Africans

and African Americans is the use of the word "black" to refer to evil and simultaneously using the same word to represent many cultures of humans. Pran lives in the mountains with her parents and younger twin brothers. Her story revolves around the conflicts and tribal wars of the area—Albanians versus Slavs and Christians versus Muslims. The girl meets and becomes enamored with Nush, who is also embroiled in the conflicts. The story evolves and Pran is betrothed to another. To protect against marrying anyone except Nush, Pran takes the vow not to marry. She wears the required men's clothing and continues to fight in the ensuing battles, believing that she will never see Nush again. Inevitably, they meet, and Nush recognizes the meaning of Pran's clothing. When asked why she made such a decision, Pran explains and, with Nush's encouragement, she speaks to a governing council regarding her rejection of a forced marriage. She is freed from her vows never to marry.

1931

Honor Award

The Dark Star of Itza: The Story of a Pagan Princess by Alida Malkus. Harcourt (out of print).

Set in Yucatán, Mexico, this story is shaped around the limited knowledge available about actual life among the Mayans. According to the author, the narrative is presented as an attempt to answer the questions: Who are the Itza? And of what race are they—Jewish, Malayan, Indian, Egyptian, or Mayan? This question asked by the author indicates the possibility of early influences in this area by Egyptians.

Ancient systems of slavery are encountered as the High Priest of Chitzen Itza and his daughter Nicté, princess of Chitzen, are spotlighted with their slaves from Toltec wars. Nicté faces being sacrificed to the well, but is saved by Itzam. A romance develops between Nicté and Itzam.

There is much here about Mayan culture and civilization, but the information does not intrude upon the reader's involvement in the princess's story of survival and love.

Ood-Le-Uk the Wanderer by Alice Lide and Margaret Johansen. Illus. by Raymond Lufkin. Little, Brown (out of print).
An informed cultural view seems evident in this title. Readers view the dangers faced by an Alaskan Inuit crossing the Bering Strait caught on an ice floe. The boy experiences his first view of a wooden house and is impressed by the lives of plenty lived by the Siberians. After years of discovery and learning, he returns to his home to establish trade between his tribe and the Siberian tribesmen. Once known as a weakling, Ood-Le-Uk becomes respected. Among the goods that were traded was a piece of green ivory carved with Ood-Le-Uk's adventures. The object becomes his mother's treasure—"the mother heart could read the history of how Ood-Le-Uk the Weakling developed into Ood-Le-Uk the Leader of Men" (265).

Queer Person by Ralph Hubbard. Doubleday.
Within cultures, prejudices often occur when one is different. A small and very odd child suddenly appears in a tribal village. He stops with one family after the other, seeking shelter and food. Far at the end of the settlement, he finally crawls in with an old woman called Granny. She accepts him, becomes his parent-guardian, and raises him. The queer one eventually becomes a part of the tribe, though his life is difficult. Granny, who is old and deserted by most of the group, struggles to keep up with the periodic movements of the tribe. She teaches Queer Person well, and finally it is the boy they called an idiot who does the bravest of deeds.

1932

Newbery Award

Waterless Mountain by Laura Adams Armer. Knopf.
Set in the 1920s, this is the timeless story of Younger Brother, an eight-year-old Navajo child. Younger Brother assumes his role within the family, herding the sheep. He has a special connection with animals and all of nature and wishes one day to become a

medicine man. To achieve this status, he must learn all the ancient customs of his tribes, about the ancestors and history. After receiving many years of training, Younger Brother accomplishes his goal. Interspersed in the boy's story are historical facts about the cultural controls and isolation of tribal groups by settlers, including information about the "Long Walk" when the Navajos were exiled to Fort Sumner in the 1860s.

Honor Award

Calico Bush by Rachel Field. Macmillan.

In colonial times, many persons of African descent served as indentured servants rather than slaves, though this kind of servitude is seen by some as equal to slavery. These servants supposedly served for a designated time period and could buy their freedom. The contracts were often broken or simply forgotten. Both African American and Caucasian indentured servants were often grossly mistreated.

Here, a French girl, Marguerite Ledoux (Maggie), becomes an indentured servant after being orphaned. Thirteen-year-old Maggie faces many trials as she serves an intolerant family in the cold wilds of Maine. An enlightening view of social and racial prejudices of the times, circa 1743.

1933

Newbery Award

Young Fu of the Upper Yangtze by Elizabeth Foreman Lewis. Winston.

The time period is about 1910 and a strong aura of European colonialism is present in this story. With a letter asking that her son, Fu Yuin-fah, be permitted to serve as an apprentice in the Tang establishment, the widowed mother Fu-Be-Be moves to Chunking with her son. The two move into a small rented room and Fu travels to the city for his apprenticeship. Fu wants to become a master coppersmith, the reason for leaving the western Chinese countryside. Amid tales of being swindled and captured and facing soldiers and thieves, Fu manages to reach his goal. He is aided by a white missionary, an old scholar, and fate.

1934

Honor Award

The Forgotten Daughter **by Caroline Snedeker. Doubleday (out of print).**
Many systems of slavery existed long before the system that brought Africans to the Americas.

Pictured in this title are two women, Chloe and Melissa, who are slaves. Vivid pictures of life in slavery are presented, including beatings. Chloe's father, a Roman centurion, has been told that his wife and child are dead and has no idea that his daughter lives a life in slavery.

Chloe falls in love with a Roman of a higher class, feeling there is no promise of their ever being together. Chloe is then forcefully betrothed to another. Later, daughter and father are reunited and the girl's real parentage is established. She and her true love, Aulus, may now be together.

1935

Honor Award

The Pageant of Chinese History **by Elizabeth Seeger. Longmans (out of print).**
It is often suggested that in early times the Chinese knew nothing of the existence of Africans. Although there are no images of Africa, this author mentions various explorers traveling to that continent. Yung-lo, the third Ming Emperor, sent a great fleet to visit the lands from China to Africa, visiting Persia and Arabia and several ports in Africa (264).

In the preface, the author laments the absence of books that detail Chinese history for young people. Provided here is an abundant view of developments in China, noting the various dynasties, art and culture, and the numerous warring tribes and invaders.

1936

Honor Award

The Good Master **by Kate Seredy. Viking.**

A strong-willed girl named Kate comes to live under the guidance of her uncle, the good master. She proves to be quite a handful but also a charmer. The book is set in Hungary prior to World War I. The lives of characters around the Hungarian ranch will be interesting to readers, as will the escapades of Kate and her cousin, Jancsi.

There are no images of persons of African descent in this book, but the people of color are Gypsies, who visit the Hungarian plains yearly. They are described as having "dark faces and piercing eyes" and the children as "clad in their own glistening brown skins and very little else . . . carefree and friendly, like a bunch of puppies" (144). This text relegates persons of color to a lesser status and carelessly refers to other humans as "puppies."

1941

Newbery Award

Call It Courage **by Armstrong Sperry. Macmillan.**

Young people are often unaware that Polynesian and Micronesian islands are populated by many persons of darker color. Arguments remain about their relationship to Africa. Over the years, some popular movies and television shows have focused on the whiter populations. This story set in Polynesia portrays a young boy, who has fears of the sea, facing a series of adventures that eventually lead to ocean encounters and the conquering of his demons. Mafatu remembers the time when at the age of three he and his mother were caught in a great storm. Their boat capsized, but his mother managed to drag him safely to a piece of coral. He lives, but she died. At the age of twelve, the son of the island's chief sets out to sea alone.

Honor Award

Young Mac of Fort Vancouver **by Mary Jane Carr. Illus. by Richard Holberg. Crowell (out of print).**

Slavery existed among tribal groups on the American continent, not to be compared with slavery perpetuated upon Africans by Europeans. In this book, a young boy accidentally releases Mia, a young slave girl, from a local tribe. This incident presents a problem in tribal versus settler relationships but is resolved when the troublemaking tribe is forced to move on to another area.

Part Cree and part French, Donald MacDermott is always afraid but eventually gains enough courage to earn the "feather of the Northmen." The story is about MacDermott's growth, his adventures at Fort Vancouver, and his interaction with tribal groups. Later in life, Mia and Donald meet again.

1945

Honor Award

Lone Journey: The Life of Roger Williams **by Jeanette Eaton. Harcourt (out of print).**

Few readers may be familiar with Roger Williams. This biography recognizes him as one of the more important contributors to the development of the democratic processes in America and for having won the battle for religious freedom. The development of life and politics in Rhode Island is the focus.

Williams struggles to save his local government and others from the formation of laws and governance that would lead America to becoming a theocracy. He fights battles to separate religious matters from civil ones. The persecution of Quakers, some of whom are ultimately hanged, is a vivid part of his story. Several Newbery choices make young people aware of Quakers but not in such detail. Williams's writings sometimes deal with race prejudice but mostly are focused on the rights of tribal members.

1946

Honor Award

The Moved-Outers **by Florence Crannell Means. Houghton.**
    Rejection and isolation of an entire cultural group is the theme of a poignant offering regarding Japanese relocation during World War II. A Japanese American family vividly describes their feelings of resignation and betrayal. Sumiko Ohara and family are first moved to the Santa Anita Race Track and then moved again to camp. The crowded and rudimentary conditions of the camp are described. Some whites are sympathetic, but others use the negative term "Japs" and figure that the suffering of their neighbors is for the good of the country.

1951

Honor Award

Better Known as Johnny Appleseed **by Mabel Leigh Hunt. Lippincott (out of print).**
    In this title, no serious images of African Americans are presented; however, there is casual mention of *negro* servants or attendants on page 90.
    Not much is recorded about the legendary figure we know as Johnny Appleseed. Mabel Leigh Hunt uses what meager information she is able to uncover to shape this fiction story about Johnny Chapman, born the son of Elizabeth and Nathaniel Chapman. Using the real aspects of places and time, and the little available information, the writer offers readers a fleshed-out person whose concern for nature makes him an oddball. Like Thoreau, Chapman encourages people to view, explore, and be involved in nature.

There are nine stories named after apples that Johnny may have planted throughout the Midwest.

1953

Newbery Award

Secret of the Andes **by Ann Nolan Clark. Viking.**
Cultural respect and spiritual information have a strong presence in this story of a young Inca boy, descendant of Mayan royalty. He learns from an elder about his heritage and his responsibility to preserve Mayan history. Cusi, the boy, lives with his guardian, Chuto, in Hidden Valley, high in the Andes. Cusi learns about his history and people as they tend a herd of llamas. Many specific cultural notes are included. This was probably the author's intention.

Honor Award

Moccasin Trail **by Eloise Jarvis McGraw. Coward.**
Cultural respect is at issue in this narrative of a young boy, Jim, living with his family on a farm in Oregon. He runs away and lives for a time with a mountain man and later spends time with tribal groups, adopting their way of life but without the respect you would assume. He later returns to his Oregon home.

When the boy Dan'l attempts to imitate Jim's life by running away, Jim rescues the boy and returns him to his family. Jim is somewhat haunted by mental reverberations of tribal medicines and the "Indian song" that have saved him in his travels, but he is chided to turn from these to the Bible.

1954

Newbery Award

. . . *And Now Miguel* **by Joseph Krumgold. Crowell.**
Here, as in many books where ethnic blends are probable, some characters are described as "dark," as is the case with the

Marquez brothers, who visit each year to shear the sheep: "There are two Marquez brothers. One is Juan, who we call Johnny, and the other is Salvador . . . with them are always three or four others. . . . [One has a] dark face and a little pointy beard" (133). Writing from the point of view of Miguel, the author recounts life in a sheep-ranching Mexican family in New Mexico. There are details of raising, branding, shearing, and all that has to do with life on the ranch. Central to the story is Miguel's wish to be like his older brother. He dreams of traveling with the herders to the beautiful mountains that stand with majesty beyond the boundaries of the ranch.

Tradition dictates that one must reach a certain age before taking this important trip. It is one year before his designated turn to go, but Miguel can't wait. He helps on the ranch in every way that he can, hoping to prove to his father that he is old enough *now*. Finding some lost sheep and his brother's sudden induction into the army become the catalysts for Miguel's permission to take the trip.

There is much beauty in the story, in its sense of family, the boy's pride in being who he is, and the magnificent scenery of the area. The book was made into a movie in 1966.

Honor Award

***Shadrach* by Meindert DeJong. Harper.**
This is a simple story, but it may be important to mention possibly unintentional negatives that resound by innuendo. Davie, the main character, prefers receiving a gift of a *black* rabbit. While thinking about naming the pet, he remembers the story of Nebuchadnezzar, Shadrach, Meshach, and Abednego: "He thought that Shadrach must be a good *black* name—Shadrach must have got pretty black in that furnace" (4). When the rabbit finally arrives, his mother says, "It's black I hope." *"Black as sin"* is Maarten's reply (94).

Davie can't wait for the little black rabbit that his father has promised him. He thinks and dreams about the rabbit, and he gets soaking wet running for the wagon in which the Maartens will bring his present.

1955

Honor Award

The Courage of Sarah Noble **by Alice Dalgliesh. Scribner.**
    Prejudices based on mistaken fears are hard to overcome, even in the face of counterevidence, as happens in this story.
    Sarah is left with tribal friends when her father travels home to bring his wife and baby to the western settlement. Sarah learns about tribal ways and prospers greatly from her adventure being adopted by a caring family.
    Sarah's mother reacts, "'I cannot think . . . how your father could leave you alone with those savages.'"
    Sarah replies, "'But they are not savages. They are our friends and Tall John's wife takes good care of her children'" (51). In spite of both Sarah's and her father's protestations, Sarah's mother is not convinced.

1958

Honor Award

The Horsecatcher **by Mari Sandoz. Westminster.**
    In this positive portrayal of tribal culture, many details about the lives of Cheyenne people are here to learn and savor. In the story about a boy who excels at catching horses, Sandoz gives us a very strong and heroic narrative. Young Elk spends months tracking and capturing wild horses. He learns their habits and idiosyncrasies and is successful. Sandoz moves the reader quietly and with suspense through Young Elk's encounters with buffalo and with rival tribes. He survives injury and near starvation, finding resources within himself to secure food and water. On his returns to his village we learn about customs and dances.

1959

Honor Award

The Perilous Road by William O. Steele. Harcourt.
Although this is a story about life during the Civil War, there are no images of African Americans and very few mentions of slavery. The story focuses on citizen involvement in the actions of war. Chris Babson hates the Union troops because they have raided the crops and have taken all of the family's food and supplies. The soldiers have also stolen the Babsons' only horse.

His brother has joined the Northern army while Chris vows to fight for the Confederacy. Chris's reporting on the coming of a Yankee supply train confronts him with major questions when he learns that his brother will probably be with that train. Needless to say, the ensuing passages are gripping as Chris learns adult lessons about choices and decision making.

1961

Newbery Award

Island of the Blue Dolphins by Scott O'Dell. Houghton.
This popular cultural saga is one of survival. When the tribal group that lived on San Nicholas Island in the Pacific leaves the island, Karana is left behind. The story follows her miraculous survival alone. Readers will be captivated by her struggles, fights with wild dogs, and the natural beauty of the island around which dolphins swim.

1962

Honor Award

The Golden Goblet by Eloise Jarvis McGraw. Coward.
Ranofer expects to inherit the business of his father, a famous goldsmith, but after his father's death, Gebu, a half-brother, takes

over. Ranofer is treated like a slave and discovers that Gebu is dealing in goods stolen from sacred burial places. One of these is a golden goblet, which Ranofer vows to return to the queen. With the help of his true friend Heqet and "The Ancient One" he manages to escape Gebu's clutches and is rewarded by the queen.

The story is interesting but not compelling. It contains many ingredients of Egyptian culture but no glossary for unknown words.

1965

Newbery Award

Shadow of a Bull by Maia Wojciechowska. Atheneum.

Documenting a controversial element of culture, the author thoroughly acquaints the reader with the traditions of bullfighting through the tale of Manolo Olivar, who is expected to follow in the footsteps of his famous bullfighting father. He is afraid, though very prepared and talented. He is not really devoted to his inherited role. At the same time, a friend of his, not so well known, has strong desires to become a bullfighter. Manolo manages to escape from being a matador and to offer an opportunity for his friend to accomplish his dream.

Some may chafe at the violent implications of the sport, but the author emphasizes the tradition as seen by the culture involved.

1967

Honor Award

The King's Fifth by Scott O'Dell. Houghton.

O'Dell tells an unusual historical story from the point of view of a young cartographer and Spanish conquistador. Central to the development of the plot is the quest for gold in the New World.

Esteban is found in jail because he has not paid the tax levied by the king of Spain on all who find precious metals. While he is in jail, everyone is trying to force Esteban to reveal the route to his source of gold. Making a pact with his jailer, Esteban agrees to draw maps that will lead the jailer to the riches. Instead, the young cartographer writes about his previous experiences and describes how he and a small band of gold seekers searched for the "Seven Golden Cities of Cibola." They were led by a young tribal girl named Zia, whose testimony at Esteban's trial is critical.

1971

Honor Award

Sing Down the Moon **by Scott O'Dell. Houghton.**
Bright Morning, a Navajo girl, lives in Canyon De Chelly. She loves to herd sheep and likes to sit and enjoy the beautiful place in which she lives. The Spanish invade her area, and she and a friend are captured and enslaved. Later, the two of them plot and accomplish their escape, but when they arrive home, the tribe has been forced to flee. The entire tribe is captured, taken, and enslaved. Many die because of crowded and unsanitary conditions.

Bright Morning survives and is married to Tall Boy. She has a child. More than anything, she wishes to return to her place of origin—the canyon. The story follows the young woman, her child, and her husband as they take the hazardous trip and finally find safety in a hidden cave.

The postscript notes that the story is based on real historical events in the history of the Navajo tribe. The three-hundred-mile journey from their land to Fort Sumner, where they were held captive, is called the Long Walk.

1973

Newbery Award

Julie of the Wolves **by Jean Craighead George. Harper.**
This title contains positive views of nature and culture. Miyax, an Inuit girl, asserts her independence and runs away from her

village. She connects with and lives as part of a wolf pack. Many details are given about the lives, habits, and group formations of the wolves, which Miyax (Julie) has an uncanny way of sensing. This is a beautiful story for those who seek books about strong, inventive females. The book is divided into three parts, "Amaroq, the Wolf," in which Miyax learns about the wolves, their language, and physical methods of communication; "Miyax the Girl," recounting the girl's happy childhood, her father going to war and being presumed dead, being betrothed to David, whom she did not love or respect, and eventually running away; and the last section, "Kapugen, the Hunter," when her beloved father returns, having married again, and Miyax has to decide if she will be part of the family.

1976

Honor Award

Dragonwings by Laurence Yep. Harper.

In a postscript, the author warns readers that his story is more of a historical fantasy than factual history. He tells a very interesting story of a young boy from China adjusting to prejudice and life with the "demons" in San Francisco.

There is much to learn about the times, the struggles of Chinese immigrants, internal fights in the Chinese cultural community, and so on. Mostly the reader is involved in the fears, fights, and adventures of the young boy. Also in the background is his father's continuing dream of flying a huge kite he is building called Dragonwings. According to the author's notes, there is some evidence of a Chinese man who did indeed make such a flight.

Provided are scenes of the great fire and also a friendship with "demons." The woman from whom they eventually rent a garage home is generous and accepting of the father and son, though this attitude is not common.

1980

Honor Award

The Road from Home: The Story of an Armenian Girl by
David Kherdian. Greenwillow.
Attempts at cultural and religious annihilation continue in
areas of the world. In this narrative, readers will learn much about
the battles between the Turks and Armenians, the massacre of Ar-
menians, being a refugee, and the life of one living in an area of war
and conflict. Few stories cover these tragic times in history. Vernon
Dumejian loves her family and the home with gardens of poppies.
She is eight years old when World War I precipitates the Turkish
repression of Armenians. Her father is called into the Turkish army.
Annihilation of Armenians continues as many are forced into the
Syrian desert. Slowly Vernon loses all her family and ends up in an
orphanage.
It is almost a miracle that Vernon is finally able to return to
her village but not to her original home. Nothing is the same. Her
grandmother still lives in the village, but as even more atrocities
come, it is her aunt with whom she finds survival.

1981

Honor Award

A Ring of Endless Light by Madeleine L'Engle. Farrar,
Straus & Giroux.
Although this narrative has no characters of color, there is one
mention of the grandfather collecting stories about Africa in order
to have these cultures preserved and remembered. Otherwise, this
complex novel for young adults deals with adolescent growth but
centers on facing death. Fifteen-year-old Vicky Austin and her
family spend the summer on Seven Bay Island with her grandfather, who is dying of leukemia. She attends the funeral of the local
Commander Rodney, where she meets Zachary, her beau from
last year's island visit. The family dislikes Zachary and later Vicky

discovers that he is inadvertently responsible for the commander's death. Zachary feels little remorse.

Vicky's love relationships are complicated by meeting Adam, who has emotional problems of his own but does fascinating work with dolphins. He is interested in dolphin-to-human communication (ESP). Adam discovers Vicky has that special connection with the dolphins that few humans are able to accomplish. Also, there is Leo, the son of Commander Rodney, who leans on Vicky after his loss.

In the meantime Grandfather has episodes that demand his being transfused. He and Vicky have established a strong rapport as he grows obviously weaker.

One evening when her grandfather's condition becomes critical, Vicky enlists Zachary's aid. He takes her to the hospital only to later desert her. In the hospital waiting room, the anxious girl meets a mother and her daughter named Binnie. Binnie's illness is critical because her father has barred her treatments. While her mother searches for a nurse, the child is left with Vicky and dies. All of this trauma leaves Vicky in a nearly catatonic state, but Adam comes to her rescue by taking her to the dolphins. The dolphins lead her back to the *light*.

1984

Honor Award

***The Sign of the Beaver* by Elizabeth George Speare. Houghton.**

This title presents the formation of an unlikely intercultural friendship. Thirteen-year-old Matt and his father build a cottage for the family in Maine. They respect the tribes who reside nearby. Father leaves Matt to care for their new home and the crops while he retrieves the rest of the family. A rifle is left for Matt's protection. When the rifle is stolen, Matt is left vulnerable. He encounters many hazards, including a bear who steals his food reserves. When seeking for honey in a tree, Matt is attacked by bees and dives into the lake to get rid of them. He is saved by the local tribe. They treat his stings and nurse him back to health. Matt is grateful and offers to give them his book, *Robinson Crusoe*. Instead of accepting the gift, the chief asks Matt to teach his grandson, Attean, to read. The relationship between Attean and Matt is tenuous in the beginning, but eventually they begin to like each other. Before Matt's family returns, the tribe moves on and Matt is invited to travel with them. He decides to continue the wait. To seal their friendship, he gives Attean his watch and Attean leaves Matt his dog.

1994

Honor Award

Dragon's Gate **by Laurence Yep. HarperCollins.**
    A gripping novel about the historical immigration of the Chinese to California and the West. The author offers details about the social prejudices and conflicts faced by Chinese workers building the transcontinental railroad.
    Otter accidentally finds himself traveling to the West, where he joins his father and uncle. Through the experiences of these three, a vivid view of the hardships encountered is presented along with historical notes about developments in China during that period.

2000

Honor Award

Our Only May Amelia **by Jennifer L. Holm. HarperCollins.**
    One mention of a "Negro" was found in this historical novel about a Finnish family that settled in coastal Washington State on the Nasel River. May Amelia is an only girl with seven brothers. She wishes for a sister and a baby is on the way. May is known to be "not a proper lady" because she never wears dresses and does what is considered boy's work around the farm. The story details elements of the Finnish culture as it explores May Amelia's emotions and

growth. Some tidbits of local tribal culture are included and a brief look at the Chinese who are smuggled in as workers is offered.

2002

Newbery Award

A Single Shard **by Linda Sue Park. Clarion Books/Houghton Mifflin.**
Cultural views and information are provided in this appealing story of "Tree-ear," an orphan who lives with "Crane-man" under a bridge. Crane-man becomes the boy's only family, the father he never knew. The two live a life of meager subsistence under the bridge, foraging for food in the woods and the garbage of villagers nearby. By accident, Tree-ear finds a way to work for "Min," one of the village of Ch'ulp'o's master potters. From the day he begins work for Min, Tree-ear and Crane-man never want for food. Although there is no pay for his work, Tree-ear receives one meal, which he shares with Crane-man.

As the captivating story evolves, Min's wife becomes attached to Tree-ear and gradually Min also begins to trust the boy. Eventually, it is Tree-ear who is responsible for Min's receipt of a royal commission for his pottery. Crane-man dies while Tree-ear is on a journey to present Min's pottery to royalty. Upon his return, the boy becomes a part of Min's family.

2003

Newbery Award

Crispin: The Cross of Lead **by Avi. Hyperion Books for Children.**
Set in fourteenth-century England, the story of Crispin reveals the gravity of serfdom and politics of feudal England. When the story begins, Crispin's mother has just died and his life becomes encumbered by a series of horrors that are linked to the church and

the man who was his father. The reader is introduced to a social system that complies with a system of slavery. The weakness of the church's moral position in these circumstances is evident as also is the seductiveness of social power. No characters are identifiably of African descent, but there is one passing mention of "Moors."

Honor Award

Surviving the Applewhites **by Stephanie S. Tolan. Harper-Collins.**

In North Carolina, Jake Semple, an incorrigible, is sent to live with a flamboyant family, the Applewhites. The Applewhites home-school their children, and they are artists and performers. Jake has been barred from all other schools because he tried to burn one down. The eccentric behaviors of the family members, Jake's growing attachment to Winston the dog, his caring for four-year-old Destiny, and the blossoming of his own creativity after being cast in the play *The Sound of Music* are all reasons for the newcomer beginning to find himself and his "passion" in life.

The story is sometimes funny and sometimes introspective. Although there are no characters of African descent, this book can be noted for at least making a nondidactic plea for multiculturalism as actors in the play are noted to be Black and Asian. When confronted about the fact that the von Trapps were all of one culture, the producer simply states that once the music starts and the play is under way, people will no longer be aware of color. For the most part, the story is just plain crazy fun.

2005

Newbery Award

Kira-Kira **by Cynthia Kadohata. Atheneum Books for Young Readers/Simon & Schuster.**

"Kira-Kira" is the song sung to Katie by her sister, Lynn, when Katie was too young to talk. Katie's older sister is her best friend and helps her understand why people stare at them when they walk

the streets. After moving from Chicago to Georgia, their father becomes a chicken sexer, but the family is poor and faces prejudices
and hard times. The girls experience what it means to be different
and wish for acceptance in the schools and neighborhood. This
Japanese family is referred to as "Indian" in one scene, when being
told they must sleep in the back rooms of a motel.

Later, after the family has made some adjustments, Lynn becomes ill. Gradually, it is learned that the illness is life threatening, and Katie loses her sister and best friend. Although set in the
South, there is no mention of African Americans, except a brief
reference made to "colored" drinking fountains, which the Japanese
were also expected to use.

2007

Honor Award

Hattie Big Sky by Kirby Larson. Delacorte.

Upon first introduction, one could assume that this is another
adventure in homesteading and moving west, about which there
are plenty of stories. Cultural prejudices are at the forefront as this
novel about Hattie develops. We meet an orphaned young woman
feeling unwanted by those who have become her caretakers. She
is bequeathed a homestead in Montana and, having no idea what
she is facing, decides to take the gift, hoping to at last have her
own home. The struggle to set up and save the homestead is only
part of the story, set during World War I. As furor against Germans
begins to brew, readers must grapple with the process by which
communities can become vindictive and turn against each other.
A young couple have befriended Hattie from the beginning—Karl
and Perilee. They have a family of three children and live nearby.
Because Karl is of German descent, the pair are targeted by the
racially intolerant and supposedly ultrapatriotic group that has been
formed. The young family has their barn burned, and Perilee, who
is pregnant, is rejected by the womenfolk.

Other characters add color and detail to the story, while Hattie's letters to her old friend Charlie add even another dimension.

Complicating all of this is a young, handsome settler, part of the marauding group. He is enamored with Hattie and seeks to buy her claim for a cattle ranch. In the end, Hattie loses the claim but gains her self-confidence and moves away to pursue a relationship with Charlie, who has returned from the war. This is compelling writing that has something of interest for all young adult readers.

Reviews:
Other Newbery
Award Winners

MANY OF THE TOP YEARLY AWARD WINNERS are reviewed in previous chapters. Those remaining cover a large number of subjects. Approximately six titles are fantasies or science fiction fantasies. There is one doll story among the fantasies and one about a pigeon in India. Four titles are set in medieval times, but each has a different focus. One book, set in Holland, is both a school and nature story. Young people dealing with problems of divorce, sibling rivalry, friendships, fears of loss, living in poverty, mental retardation, and self-esteem issues are themes of several. One family story deals with adjustments in the aftermath of the Vietnam War. Five of the remaining winners are animal stories or animal fantasies and two deal with the death of a friend or parent. Refreshingly, there are two books of poetry that were winners, and the most current winner is a novel about a young boy being raised in a graveyard. Reviews of these winners are provided as an opportunity to appreciate the myriad of subjects that are dealt with in these selections while thus far the concentration has been upon views of Africans, African Americans, and other selected cultural groups. No books receiving honor awards are included in the reviews that follow.

1924

The Dark Frigate **by Charles Boardman Hawes. Little, Brown.**

Philip Marsham runs away from home and school to join his father, who sails aboard the ketch *Sarah*. Because Philip falls ill, he is not aboard when the ketch is lost at sea. Orphaned and pursued because of a gun accident, he runs again and eventually sails on *The Rose of Devon*. The ship is captured by pirates and Philip is forced to participate in the dastardly acts of his captors. There are love interests and other adventures, but none end happily.

The writer compels readers to become involved with the protagonist, and as he escapes one adventure and misadventure after another, one wonders, "What else?"

1928

Gay-Neck: The Story of a Pigeon **by Dhan Gopal Mukerji. Dutton (out of print).**

A pigeon, lovingly cared for, is owned by Mukerji, a young boy in India. The pigeon is named Chitra (painted in gay colors) griva (neck). The story is told alternately from the point of view of the pigeon and that of the humans. The pigeon fears hawk, who has killed one of his parents, and fleeing the dreaded predator, Gay-Neck finds himself living in a lamasery with Buddhist monks. The pigeon returns home, only to leave again. Gay-Neck joins Ghond the Hunter and travels to Europe, where the pigeon becomes a messenger. There are scenes of and insights into the trauma of war, which leaves both the pigeon and Ghond battered. After a time of healing, the pigeon again returns home.

1929

The Trumpeter of Krakow **by Eric P. Kelly. Macmillan.**

A fictional story about the historical fire that burned most of Krakow in 1462. Father Andrew moves his family to Krakow just in time to escape thieves seeking the crystal in his care. A complicated story evolves as the father and his son, Joseph, become involved in saving the city. The title is based on a story told by the boy's father when they visit the tower of the Church of Our Lady. In the past a trumpeter was pierced by an arrow before he could finish the Hejnal; since that time the song has been abruptly cut short. This becomes the clue for survival.

1931

The Cat Who Went to Heaven by Elizabeth Coatsworth. Macmillan.

When a poor Japanese painter sends his housekeeper to buy food, she returns with a small white cat, declaring that their home is too lonely. The painter is temporarily angry, but noticing the cat's good behavior, he soon changes his mind. The little cat prays to Buddha and has almost human behavior. When the painter is commissioned to paint a picture of the death of Buddha, he is paid a good sum but does not feel fulfilled. He completes the picture of Buddha with animals pictured except for a cat. Tradition says Buddha rejected cats. When the picture is completed, the dying housekeeper requests that the cat be added to the picture. The painter fulfills her request, but when the people see the cat pictured, they are angry, until a miracle happens. The next day Buddha's hand is shown blessing the little cat.

1938

The White Stag by Kate Seredy. Viking.

A mythical story of the Huns and Magyars who traveled across Asia to Europe, always following the White Stag. The promised land that they eventually find is Hungary. The story also presents a fanciful picture of Attila the Hun (The Red Eagle).

1939

***Thimble Summer* by Elizabeth Enright. Holt.**

A feisty farm girl named Garnet, the main character, finds a silver thimble. She is convinced that the thimble's power changes the plight of her family, ends a terrible drought, and brings her luck. On this basis, the reader is treated to a summer of fun and trials, and there is much to learn about country life and pleasures. The title is explained when Garnet tells Eric about her thimble, how she found it, and all the good things that happened afterward: "As long as I live, I'm always going to call this summer the thimble summer" (123).

1943

***Adam of the Road* by Elizabeth Janet Gray. Illus. by Robert Lawson. Viking.**

Adam is a budding minstrel, whose minstrel father is well known. He has been left by his father at a monastery school, where he is lonely except for his friend Perkins and a dog. The dog, Nick, is not allowed at the abbey but is kept by a kindly woman nearby. Whenever possible, Adam visits and plays with the dog.

When his father, Roger, returns, Adam is able to leave the school and travel as a minstrel's apprentice. The rest of the story involves those travels, which are enjoyable and sometimes perilous. Adam insists upon taking the small dog along, and many people are captivated by the dog's charm and ability to walk on two legs. The dog is stolen, and Adam is lost from his father, but the boy continues his travels and searches for the two. Exciting events occur during these travels, including Adam being chased and arrested. All ends well, and Adam, Nick, and Roger are eventually reunited. This story is still fun to read, especially for those interested in life during medieval times.

1945

Rabbit Hill by Robert Lawson. Viking.
A delightful story that characterizes a group of animals waiting for the arrival of the family that will live on the hill. The family proves more than accommodating to the needs of the animals. They hang a sign that says, "Please Drive Carefully on Account of Small Animals." The animals overhear them saying there will be no traps or poison. When one of the animals, "Little George," is injured and presumed dead, it is discovered that he is being nursed back to health in the house on the hill.

1947

Miss Hickory by Carolyn Sherwin Bailey with lithographs by Ruth Gannett. Viking.
Miss Hickory is a doll made with the body of an apple-wood twig and the head of a hickory nut. When she receives the news that the family who cares for her is moving away, she can't believe it. After discovering the rumor is true, Miss Hickory is given help by Crow and manages to survive most of the winter living in a nest deserted by robins. She spends moments of enjoyment with the animals, and her only threat is Squirrel, whom she doesn't trust. Squirrel is kept at bay for some time, until his greed overwhelms him and he snatches Miss Hickory's head and eats it. The headless doll wanders to an apple tree where she goes to sleep and becomes a scion, living again as part of the apple tree near the home of those she loves.

Young children may not understand the symbolism of "life after death" and become distressed when the doll's head is eaten.

1948

The Twenty-One Balloons by William Pene du Bois. Viking.
With the appearance of a colorful picture book, this story is of a retired teacher who begins a trip around the world in a balloon. Life

aboard is described humorously, as is the balloon's crash landing on Krakatoa. An escape is managed before the famous explosion. The book is brief with pictures that are meant to provoke humor.

1950

The Door in the Wall by Marguerite de Angeli. Doubleday.
Set in the Middle Ages, this is the saga of Robin, whose father has left to fight the Scots and whose mother is called away to serve the queen. Robin suffers an illness that leaves his legs quite crippled. He is left alone by the servants, deserted and helpless. Brother Luke, a monk, rescues Robin and carries him to safety. Later the castle comes under attack, and it is Robin, in spite of his handicap, who saves the day. His mother returns and Robin is recognized as a hero.

The book's title derives from words of encouragement said to Robin by the monk: "Thou hast only to follow the wall far enough and there will be a door in it."

1955

The Wheel on the School by Meindert DeJong. Harper.
Young children in a Dutch village search for wagon wheels. Their hope is to place the wheels on the roof of the schoolhouse in order to attract storks. Lisa, who has wondered why no storks come to Shora and build nests, learns that the roofs of buildings are too steep. The solution is to place wheels on the roof in which the storks can build their nests. Lisa and the other schoolchildren search for wheels that will fit this task. Two storks are saved from a storm, but no wheel is yet available to them for nesting. Mildly humorous incidents regarding the efforts to find the right wheel follow.

1957

Miracles on Maple Hill by Virginia Sorensen. Harcourt.
After the war and experience as a P.O.W., the father of Marly and Joe returns very disturbed and alienated from his family.

Mother decides that it might be good therapy to visit their rural farm in Pennsylvania. Father thrives in this setting and decides to stay while the family visits on weekends. Later they all move to this place, which provides so much healing for the father that the family becomes reconciled. Marly and Joe also enjoy living in this new setting with a new school and new friends. Their adventures and information about the area are provided.

Details are shared about the gathering and processing of maple syrup and added to this are suspense and mystery on the night when Joe can't be found.

1963

A Wrinkle in Time by Madeleine L'Engle. Farrar.
Through a science fiction story, questions are posed that could apply to real-life situations. Meg Murry's father has been captured and imprisoned in space by the IT. With her brother and a friend, Meg travels into space to free her father. Mrs. Whatsit, who looks like a tramp, arrives at the Murry home one evening to inform the mother that tesseracts (wrinkles in time) do exist. It is through this wrinkle that Meg travels. The travel through space and time, battles with the IT, hair-raising escapes, and the eventual conquering of the IT with *Love* complete this popular science fiction fantasy.

1968

From the Mixed-Up Files of Mrs. Basil E. Frankweiler by E. L. Konigsburg. Atheneum.
Readers will be engaged by this story of two runaways who hide out in a most unlikely place. Claudia has carefully planned to run away and has decided that in order to be successful, she will need the assistance of her frugal, penny-saving younger brother. The escapade is planned to teach Claudia's parents that she needs more appreciation.

Brother and sister hide out in New York's Metropolitan Museum. There enters the mystery regarding the identity of the sculptor of a statue recently added to the museum collection. Now the children become both runaways and sleuths, outwitting the guards in the museum as they devise their own plans to sleep and bathe. Days are spent in the city using the money Claudia and brother Jamie have saved. When the funds run low, the children take money from a fountain.

Claudia's big problem is that she wants to be different—to do something big. She does not want to return home until she solves the mystery of the sculptor. The solution is eventually found when she writes to and visits Mrs. Frankweiler, the statue's donor.

Oddly, no images of African Americans appear in this big city adventure, but such an encounter is not necessary to the story.

1969

The High King by Lloyd Alexander. Holt.

This is the fifth book in the Prydain Chronicles. Fans will enjoy continuing and final battles as the story of magic people concludes. Assistant Pig Keeper Taran realizes that his greatest wish is to marry Eilonwy. Many obstacles must be overcome as he travels with his companion Gurgi and Kaw the crow.

1971

The Summer of the Swans by Betsy Byars. Viking.

Another story presents the challenges of adolescence and the opportunities to grow and become a better person. Sara is not pleased with her looks and her family relationships. She overprotects her mentally handicapped brother, Charlie. Charlie becomes the center for much of Sara's learning and growth.

Within many incidents at school and with family, Sara accuses everyone except herself. Because of her insecurities, she alienates friends at school. During the summer, Aunt Willy tells Sara that she is not ugly and will soon become a swan. Charlie, who is fascinated with the real swans in the area, leaves the house one evening in search of the birds. He becomes lost. Sara blames herself and tries to find her brother. It is Joe, one of Sara's former friends, who finds clues to the lost child's whereabouts. Sara, who is most acquainted with Charlie, senses where he might be and continues calling when others joining the search give up hope. During this adventure, Joe and Sara converse, revealing the girl's mistakes in blaming others. This event, with an apology and reconciliation with Joe, is the beginning of Sara's blossoming.

1972

Mrs. Frisby and the Rats of NIMH by Robert C. O'Brien. Atheneum.

Questions about genetic engineering arise in this story about a mother rat, Mrs. Frisby, planning to move her family from their summer home. When her son Timothy becomes ill with pneumonia and can't be moved, Mrs. Frisby enlists the aid of a colony of rats nearby, who are bred to be highly intelligent. The genetically altered rats escaped from a testing laboratory many years ago. Although the experiment in which they participated did not prove it, these rats developed intelligence that provides them with extraordinary survival skills. They engineer a plan to help Mrs. Frisby.

1976

The Grey King by Susan Cooper. McElderry/Atheneum.

This is one of the author's titles in the fantasy series The Dark Is Rising. Set in Wales, a boy discovers that he is one with a mission to fight the evils of the world. He is an "Old One" destined to awaken others who have the same powers. Will Stanton is sent to a farm in Wales to recuperate from hepatitis. He discovers Bran, a young albino boy with golden eyes. Bran has been left in the care of Owen Davies by Gwen, his mother. It is with Bran's powers and his own that Will accomplishes his mission of defeating the Dark.

They conquer the Grey King, the evil one who opposes the light, and huge gray foxes called milgwn, which only Bran can see.

1978

Bridge to Terabithia by Katherine Paterson. Crowell.

Jesse Aarons discovers that his new neighbor, Leslie Burkes, is an unusual person when she beats him at a footrace and then introduces him to her magical kingdom of Terabithia. The two spend many days escaping to their kingdom, with the realism of family and school in the background.

Leslie's tragic death provides the reader with a stark view of life and death happening among the young. Jesse's struggles with grief are difficult but in the end help him to grow stronger.

This story has been made into two movies, one in 1985 and another in 2007.

1981

Jacob Have I Loved by Katherine Paterson. Crowell.

Set on an island in the Chesapeake Bay, the story of Louise and the Bradshaws is one of sibling rivalry and adult insensitivity.

Louise lives in the shadow of her sister, Caroline, who is a talented musician. As attention is paid to Caroline's progress and needs, Louise is regularly ignored. Sacrifices are made to send Caroline to school at Juilliard to begin her music career, while Louise is left pretty much to fend for herself.

There is another story integrated into Louise's saga, one of an older man who appears on the scene. It is revealed that this man was the grandmother's past love. It is grandmother who refers Louise to the Bible story of Jacob and Esau, from which the title comes.

Caroline seems to receive all rewards, including the young man named "Call," with whom Louise has had a major relationship. In the end, of course, Louise comes into her own and leaves the island. Unlike many other stories for young people, this one follows Louise into adulthood, eventual marriage, and having children.

1982

A Visit to William Blake's Inn: Poems for Innocent and Experienced Travelers by Nancy Willard. Harcourt.
Through a series of poems by Blake, readers visit an inn. A child visiting the inn discovers colorful inhabitants such as Rabbit, Rat, and the Man in the Marmalade Hat. Blake's simply written poems are about wonder and magic and the beauties of nature and the universe.

1984

Dear Mr. Henshaw by Beverly Cleary. Morrow.
A young boy having problems facing his parents' divorce writes letters to an author, Mr. Henshaw. The author provides advice about writing and the boy learns lessons about the creative process and about life. The first letters are written to the real Mr. Henshaw and later ones are entries in a diary.

1985

The Hero and the Crown by Robin McKinley. Greenwillow.
The Hero and the Crown is a fantasy whose main character is Aerin, daughter of Arlbeth, king of Damar. With pale skin and fiery hair, Aerin looks different from others in her kingdom, most of whom have dark hair and skin. While growing up, the king's daughter is taunted by rumors that her mother was a witch and that she is not of royal blood, but one of her friends and strongest supporters is Tor. Aerin learns to ride Talat, her father's old warhorse,

and discovers a method for making an ointment that will protect her from fire. After becoming a dragon slayer, Aerin gains little respect from her people, although she saves many. The rest of the story is a complex set of events, including attempts to defeat the conquering northerners, Aerin's injury and long illmess, dreams that lure Aerin to a healer, and finally a battle for the king's crown. In the end, Arlbeth dies, and Aerin marries Tor. At long last she has gained the respect of her people.

1986

Sarah, Plain and Tall by Patricia MacLachlan. Harper.

After Mother dies, Papa is sad and the children are lonely for a woman's presence. Papa puts an ad in the paper and receives an answer from Sarah. They all write back and soon Sarah decides to come for a month. It is Sarah who describes herself by letter as "plain and tall."

When she arrives, the children like her a lot, but they are not sure if she and their papa will like each other or if Sarah will like them. The youngsters do everything they can think of to make her stay.

1987

The Whipping Boy by Sid Fleischman. Greenwillow.

Apparently based on an ancient custom, the whipping boy is one who takes punishment when a privileged one has done wrong. In this fable, the two boys exchange places and each learns about the other's circumstance. Prince Brat, the king's son, and Jemmy, orphaned son of the rat catcher, run away together and are soon captured by two well-known outlaws. Jemmy convinces them that he is the real prince because he is the one who can read and write. It is also Jemmy who orchestrates an escape. There are some entertaining and humorous moments but hardly captivating.

1989

Joyful Noise: Poems for Two Voices by Paul Fleischman. Harper.
It is always refreshing to see a book of poetry win in the Newbery category. Young people of all ages could be encouraged to present aloud these poems, which are both entertaining and humorous.

1990

Number the Stars by Lois Lowry. Houghton.
Set in 1943, during the Nazi occupation of Denmark, the story is of two friends. Ellen Rosen is Jewish and Annemarie Johansen is Danish. The Danish family harbors the Jewish one from the Nazis. Recorded is the bravery of adults, children, and underground workers under Nazi threat. Danish residents develop a system by which Jewish families are transported by boat (hidden in secret compartments) to safety in Sweden.
Told by ten-year-old Annemarie, the events amplify the Danish role in smuggling approximately seven thousand people into Sweden. A tribute to the human spirit, this is a worthwhile addition to several novels for the young documenting this historical period.

1992

Shiloh by Phyllis Reynolds Naylor. Atheneum.
Marty engages a beagle in the woods and would like to keep him, but his father insists that the dog be returned to his owner. Marty is devastated when he discovers that Judd, the owner, mistreats the dog. The remainder of the story recounts Marty's embattlement with the mean owner and efforts to save the beagle, which the boy has named Shiloh.

1993

***Missing May* by Cynthia Rylant. Jackson/Orchard.**
Summer shares the story of her journey through grief after her
Aunt May dies. Aunt May and Uncle Ob raised Summer in a little
trailer in West Virginia. The narrative reveals memories of great
happiness and the child's observations of love and commitment
between the aunt and uncle.

During the period of grief, a young boy named Cletus Under-
wood enters the picture. It is he who assists in removing the chasm
that has formed between Summer and her uncle as they both dealt
individually with missing May.

1994

***The Giver* by Lois Lowry. Houghton.**
In an imaginary community where all developments and people
are controlled, there lives a young boy aged eleven about to turn
twelve. Jonas suffers anxiety about the ceremony for those who
become "twelves." It is at that time when life changes from that of
a child to being assigned one's life's work. At the ceremony, Jonas
is given the highest designation of the "Receiver," while the man
designated to train him for this role becomes the "Giver."

Controls on the community have eliminated colors, music, and
love, but as the Receiver, Jonas is exposed to such things. Soon realizing that rigid community controls are governed by lies, he decides
to escape, taking along Gabriel, a baby designated to die.

1995

***Walk Two Moons* by Sharon Creech. HarperCollins.**
Salamanca travels from Ohio to Idaho with her colorful grandparents, with whom she lives because her mother has left the
family. There are adventures and misadventures on the trip while
Salamanca tells her grandparents the saga of Phoebe Winterbot-

tom, whose mother disappears. The multilayered story reveals the complexity of broken family relationships and the struggles to mend them. All is seen through the eyes of a young girl proud of her "Indian" heritage. Included are adventure, humor, tragedy, and the eventual discovery of the fate of Salamanca's mother.

1996

The Midwife's Apprentice **by Karen Cushman. Clarion.**

Set in England in the fourteenth century, this is the story of one waif named Alyce, among the many poverty-stricken, parentless children of that time. Formerly named Beetle, Alyce, who decides to change her name, survives and later prospers by becoming an apprentice to the village midwife. She is the apprentice of Jane Sharp, a skilled but rigid taskmaster. Alyce learns well and on one occasion manages a delivery on her own, when Jane has to be absent. Detailed descriptions of the life and work are offered.

1997

The View from Saturday **by E. L. Konigsburg. Jean Karl/ Atheneum.**

Presented here are adventures of the academic bowl team from the sixth grade at Epiphany Middle School. They are described in the text as "one Jew, one half-Jew, a WASP and an Indian [East Indian]." The secondary stories are those of team participants and that of Ms. Olinski, the paraplegic teacher and team leader. The team are eventual winners in more ways than mastering the academic tests.

1998

Out of the Dust **by Karen Hesse. Scholastic.**

A poetic, lyrical, painfully revealing story of the Oklahoma "dust bowl" during the Great Depression. Symbolic of the greater tragedies facing numbers of people at that time are the series of events that touch the life of the main character and her family. The physical and emotional struggles she gradually overcomes during this period are compelling. Fourteen-year-old Billie Jo through verse makes the reader taste the dust that buried everything, including her beloved piano. We are numbed by the violent accident in which her mother is killed and Billie Jo's hands so injured she may never play again. Sorrow is deeply felt for the child and her father, who is slowly dying before her eyes. We can only wonder and hope that her life will be better when she jumps a train and heads west.

2001

A Year Down Yonder by Richard Peck. Dial.

Set in 1937 during a recession reminiscent of the Great Depression, which has just ended, this is the story of fifteen-year-old Mary Alice. The child is sent to live with her grandmother because there is no money nor space to live with her parents. Mary Alice moves reluctantly to her grandmother's small-town Illinois home. Life with Grandma reveals a feisty woman, whom granddaughter Mary Alice begins to admire in that one year. Other encounters, local celebrations, school intrigue, and small-town pretentiousness add to an entertaining story.

2004

The Tale of Despereaux: Being the Story of a Mouse, a Princess, Some Soup, and a Spool of Thread by Kate DiCamillo. Illus. by Timothy Basil Ering. Candlewick Press.

In this fantasy adventure of animals, mice and rats interact with humans, complete with castles, dungeons, and heroic cooks. The mouse with big ears is in love with a princess named Pea. He is banished to the dungeon because of his love of the princess, music, and other elements of culture. In the dungeon live the rats who kill. Also, there is Miggery, the girl who has been traded into servitude by her own father. The fantasy becomes one of dangers, escapes, and love.

2006

Criss Cross by Lynne Rae Perkins. Greenwillow Books/ HarperCollins.
   A young adult story about growing up and first loves, the book is narrated by two fourteen-year-olds, Debbie and Hector. Debbie wishes that something different would happen in her life, while Hector, a distinctive and humorous character, also faces the "crossroads" of growing up. The author combines traditional elements of young adult struggles, insecurities, and romantic crushes with introspection through poetry and haiku. These young adult character studies should have wide appeal.

2007

The Higher Power of Lucky by Susan Patron. Illus. by Matt Phelan. Simon & Schuster/Richard Jackson.
   Ten-year-old Lucky calls upon her "higher power" for help. After Lucky's mother dies, her father's first wife, Brigitte, moves to California from France to become the girl's guardian. Life is not easy in the desert town that is their home, and Lucky suffers from the fear that her new parent will leave her. Brigitte, her guardian, doesn't hide her longing for home in Paris. Lucky decides to run away with her dog. After some introspection, Lucky throws away the ashes of her mother, which she has kept all this time. Returning home she finds that Brigitte was preparing to adopt her.

2008

Good Masters! Sweet Ladies! Voices from a Medieval Village by Laura Amy Schlitz. Candlewick.
   An illustrated, poetic presentation of characters from medieval years. Each poem offers some detail of life during the times. Occasionally interspersed are pages containing historical notes regarding this period, such as one giving background about the Crusades.

2009

The Graveyard Book by Neil Gaiman. Illus. by Dave McKean. HarperCollins.

One night the killer Jack with a sharp knife destroys all of a family except the baby, who is missing from his crib in an upstairs room. The baby has the habit of climbing out of his crib and walking. He has found his way to the graveyard. There, the orphaned boy is adopted by the ghosts of Mr. and Mrs. Owens, married two hundred and fifty years with no children of their own. The graveyard fantasy-adventure begins. The boy is welcomed in the hill graveyard and grows up with experiences with the people of the past, encounters with ghouls, and historical visits through ancient tombs and crypts. Always threatening is Jack, the killer, who given a chance would kill again. Silas, the boy's guardian, is the caretaker who travels between the living and the dead and is able to bring food and medicine.

FINAL NOTE

Progress made in the presentation of African and African American images in award selections is evident. Although there are many worthy titles found among Newbery Award selections, it should probably *not* be the first source for those seeking materials about Africans and African Americans. For teachers, parents, and others seeking a number of books that present fair and positive images of African Americans, the Coretta Scott King Book Award listing is highly recommended. This award is presented each year by the Ethnic and Multicultural Information Exchange Roundtable of the American Library Association, 50 E. Huron Street, Chicago, Illinois, 60611 (ala.org). For other lists and multicultural recommendations, contact Ms. Satia M. Orange, Director, Office for Literacy and Outreach Services (OLOS), at the American Library Association address above, or at www.ala.org/olos.

Newbery Author List

Alexander, Lloyd. *The Black Cauldron* (1966)
  The High King (1969)
Allee, Marjorie. *Jane's Island* (1932)
Angelo, Valenti. *Nino* (1939)
Appelt, Kathi. *Underneath* (2009)
Armer, Laura Adams. *Waterless Mountain* (1932)
Armstrong, Alan. *Whittington* (2006)
Armstrong, William H. *Sounder* (1970)
Atwater, Richard and Florence. *Mr. Popper's Penguins* (1939)
Avi. *Crispin: The Cross of Lead* (2003)
  Nothing But the Truth: A Documentary Novel (1992)
  The True Confessions of Charlotte Doyle (1991)
Babbitt, Natalie. *Kneeknock Rise* (1971)
Bailey, Carolyn Sherwin. *Miss Hickory* (1947)
Baity, Elizabeth. *Americans Before Columbus* (1952)
Barnes, Nancy. *Wonderful Year* (1947)
Bartoletti, Susan Campbell. *Hitler Youth: Growing Up in Hitler's Shadow* (2006)
Bauer, Joan. *Hope Was Here* (2001)
Bauer, Marion Dane. *On My Honor* (1987)
Bemelmans, Ludwig. *The Golden Basket* (1937)
Bennett, John. *The Pigtail of Ah Lee Ben Loo, with Seventeen Other Laughable Tales and 200 Comical Silhouettes* (1929)

Berry, Erick. *The Winged Girl of Knossos* (1934)

Best, Herbert. *Garram the Hunter: A Boy of the Hill Tribes* (1931)

Besterman, Catherine. *The Quaint and Curious Quest of Johnny Longfoot* (1948)

Bianco, Margery Williams. *Winterbound* (1937)

Bishop, Claire Huchet. *All Alone* (1954)
    Pancakes-Paris (1948)

Blos, Joan W. *A Gathering of Days: A New England Girl's Journal, 1830–1832* (1980)

Blumberg, Rhoda. *Commodore Perry in the Land of the Shogun* (1986)

Bond, Nancy. *A String in the Harp* (1977)

Bontemps, Arna. *Story of the Negro* (1949)

Bowen, William. *The Old Tobacco Shop: A True Account of What Befell a Little Boy in Search of Advent* (1922)

Bowman, James Cloyd. *Pecos Bill* (1938)

Brink, Carol Ryrie. *Caddie Woodlawn* (1936)

Brittain, Bill. *The Wish Giver: Three Tales of Coven Tree* (1984)

Brooks, Bruce. *The Moves Make the Man* (1985)
    What Hearts (1993)

Buff, Mary and Conrad. *The Apple and the Arrow* (1952)
    Big Tree (1947)
    Magic Maize (1954)

Burglon, Nora. *Children of the Soil: A Story of Scandinavia* (1933)

Byars, Betsy. *The Summer of the Swans* (1971)

Carlson, Natalie Savage. *The Family under the Bridge* (1959)

Carr, Mary Jane. *Young Mac of Fort Vancouver* (1941)

Caudill, Rebecca. *Tree of Freedom* (1950)

Choldenko, Gennifer. *Al Capone Does My Shirts* (2005)

Chrisman, Arthur Bowie. *Shen of the Sea* (1926)

Clark, Ann Nolan. *Secret of the Andes* (1953)

Cleary, Beverly. *Dear Mr. Henshaw* (1984)
    Ramona and Her Father (1978)
    Ramona Quimby, Age 8 (1982)

Coatsworth, Elizabeth. *The Cat Who Went to Heaven* (1931)

Coblentz, Catherine. *The Blue Cat of Castle Town* (1950)

Collier, James Lincoln and Christopher. *My Brother Sam Is Dead* (1975)

Colum, Padraic. *Big Tree of Bunlahy: Stories of My Own Country-side* (1934)

The Golden Fleece and the Heroes Who Lived Before Achilles (1922)

The Voyagers: Being Legends and Romances of Atlantic Discovery (1926)

Coman, Carolyn. *What Jamie Saw* (1996)

Conly, Jane Leslie. *Crazy Lady!* (1994)

Coolidge, Olivia. *Men of Athens* (1963)

Cooper, Susan. *The Dark Is Rising* (1974)

The Grey King (1976)

Couioumbis, Audrey. *Getting Near to Baby* (2000)

Courlander, Harold. *The Cow-Tail Switch and Other West African Stories* (1948)

Crawford, Phyllis. *Hello the Boat!* (1939)

Creech, Sharon. *Walk Two Moons* (1995)

The Wanderer (2001)

Curtis, Christopher Paul. *Bud, Not Buddy* (2000)

Elijah of Buxton (2008)

The Watsons Go to Birmingham—1963 (1996)

Cushman, Karen. *Catherine, Called Birdy* (1995)

The Midwife's Apprentice (1996)

Dalgliesh, Alice. *The Bears on Hemlock Mountain* (1953)

The Courage of Sarah Noble (1955)

The Silver Pencil (1945)

Daugherty, James. *Daniel Boone* (1940)

Davis, Julia. *Mountains Are Free* (1931)

Vaino, A Boy of New Finland (1930)

Davis, Mary Gould. *The Truce of the Wolf and Other Tales of Old Italy* (1932)

de Angeli, Marguerite. *The Black Fox of Lorne* (1957)

The Door in the Wall (1950)

DeJong, Meindert. *Along Came a Dog* (1959)

The House of Sixty Fathers (1957)

Hurry Home, Candy (1954)

Shadrach (1954)

The Wheel on the School (1955)

DePaola, Tomie. *26 Fairmont Avenue* (2000)

de Trevino, Elizabeth Borton. *I, Juan de Pareja* (1966)

DiCamillo, Kate. *Because of Winn-Dixie* (2001)

    The Tale of Despereaux: Being the Story of a Mouse, a Princess, Some Soup, and a Spool of Thread (2004)

du Bois. William Pene. *The Twenty-One Balloons* (1948)

Eaton, Jeanette. *Daughter of the Seine: The Life of Madame Roland* (1930)

    Gandhi, Fighter without a Sword (1951)

    Leader by Destiny: George Washington, Man and Patriot (1939)

    Lone Journey: The Life of Roger Williams (1945)

Eckert, Allan W. *Incident at Hawk's Hill* (1972)

Edmonds, Walter D. *The Matchlock Gun* (1942)

Engdahl, Sylvia Louise. *Enchantress from the Stars* (1971)

Engle, Margarita. *The Surrender Tree, Poems of Cuba's Struggle for Freedom* (2009)

Enright, Elizabeth. *Gone-Away Lake* (1958)

    Thimble Summer (1939)

Estes, Eleanor. *Ginger Pye* (1952)

    The Hundred Dresses (1945)

    The Middle Moffat (1943)

    Rufus M. (1944)

Farmer, Nancy. *The Ear, the Eye, and the Arm* (1995)

    A Girl Named Disaster (1997)

    The House of the Scorpion (2003)

Fenner, Carol. *Yolanda's Genius* (1996)

Field, Rachel. *Calico Bush* (1932)

    Hitty, Her First Hundred Years (1930)

Finger, Charles. *Tales from Silver Lands* (1925)

Fisher, Cyrus. *The Avion My Uncle Flew* (1947)

Fleischman, Paul. *Graven Images* (1983)

    Joyful Noise: Poems for Two Voices (1989)

Fleischman, Sid. *The Whipping Boy* (1987)

Forbes, Esther. *Johnny Tremain* (1944)

Foster, Genevieve. *Abraham Lincoln's World* (1945)

Birthdays of Freedom, Volume I (1953)
George Washington (1950)
George Washington's World (1942)
Fox, Paula. *The One-Eyed Cat* (1985)
The Slave Dancer (1974)
Freedman, Russell. *Eleanor Roosevelt: A Life of Discovery* (1994)
Lincoln: A Photobiography (1988)
The Voice that Challenged a Nation: Marian Anderson and the Struggle for Equal Rights (2005)
The Wright Brothers: How They Invented the Airplane (1992)
Fritz, Jean. *Homesick: My Own Story* (1983)
Gag, Wanda. *The ABC Bunny* (1934)
Millions of Cats (1929)
Gaggin, Eva Roe. *Down Ryton Water* (1942)
Gaiman, Neil. *The Graveyard Book* (2009)
Gannett, Ruth S. *My Father's Dragon* (1949)
Gantos, Jack. *Joey Pigza Loses Control* (2001)
Gates, Doris. *Blue Willow* (1941)
George, Jean Craighead. *Julie of the Wolves* (1973)
My Side of the Mountain (1960)
Giff, Patricia Reilly. *Lily's Crossing* (1998)
Pictures of Hollis Woods (2003)
Gipson, Fred. *Old Yeller* (1957)
Gray, Elizabeth Janet. *Adam of the Road* (1943)
Meggy MacIntosh (1931)
Penn (1939)
Young Walter Scott (1936)
Greene, Bette. *Philip Hall Likes Me, I Reckon Maybe* (1975)
Gurko, Leo. *Tom Paine, Freedom's Apostle* (1958)
Hale, Shannon. *Princess Academy* (2006)
Hall, Anna Gertrude. *Nansen* (1941)
Hallock, Grace. *The Boy Who Was* (1929)
Hamilton, Virginia. *In The Beginning: Creation Stories from Around the World* (1989)
M. C. Higgins the Great (1975)
The Planet of Junior Brown (1972)
Sweet Whispers, Brother Rush (1983)

Havighurst, Walter and Marion. *Song of the Pines: A Story of Norwegian Lumbering in Wisconsin* (1950)
Hawes, Charles Boardman. *The Dark Frigate* (1924)
    The Great Quest: A Romance of 1826 (1922)
Henkes, Kevin. *Olive's Ocean* (2004)
Henry, Marguerite. *Justin Morgan Had a Horse* (1946)
    King of the Wind (1949)
    Misty of Chincoteague (1948)
Hesse, Karen. *Out of the Dust* (1998)
Hewes, Agnes. *The Codfish Musket* (1937)
    Glory of the Seas (1934)
    Spice and the Devil's Cave (1931)
Hiaasen, Carl. *Hoot* (2003)
Highwater, Jamake. *Anpao: An American Indian Odyssey* (1978)
Holling, Holling C. *Minn of the Mississippi* (1952)
    Seabird (1949)
Holm, Jennifer L. *Our Only May Amelia* (2000)
    Penny from Heaven (2007)
Horvath, Polly. *Everything on a Waffle* (2002)
Hubbard, Ralph. *Queer Person* (1931)
Hunt, Irene. *Across Five Aprils* (1965)
    Up a Road Slowly (1967)
Hunt, Mabel Leigh. *Better Known as Johnny Appleseed* (1951)
    Have You Seen Tom Thumb? (1943)
Ish-Kishor, Sulamith. *Our Eddie* (1970)
James, Will. *Smokey the Cowhorse* (1927)
Jarrell, Randall. *The Animal Family* (1966)
Jewett, Eleanore. *The Hidden Treasure of Glaston* (1947)
Johnson, Gerald W. *America Is Born: A History for Peter* (1960)
    America Moves Forward: A History for Peter (1961)
Jones, Idwal. *Whistlers' Van* (1937)
Judson, Clara Ingram. *Abraham Lincoln, Friend of the People* (1951)
    Mr. Justice Holmes (1957)
    Theodore Roosevelt, Fighting Patriot (1954)
Jukes, Mavis. *Like Jake and Me* (1985)
Kadohata, Cynthia. *Kira-Kira* (2005)
Kalashnikoff, Nicholas. *The Defender* (1952)

Kalnay, Francis. *Chucaro: Wild Pony of the Pampa* (1959)
Keith, Harold V. *Rifles for Watie* (1958)
Kelly, Eric P. *The Trumpeter of Krakow* (1929)
Kendall, Carol. *The Gammage Cup* (1960)
Kherdian, David. *The Road from Home: The Story of an Armenian Girl* (1980)
Konigsburg, E. L. *From the Mixed-Up Files of Mrs. Basil E. Frankweiler* (1968)
    Jennifer, Hecate, Macbeth, William McKinley, and Me, Elizabeth (1968)
    The View from Saturday (1997)
Krumgold, Joseph. *. . . And Now Miguel* (1954)
    Onion John (1960)
Kyle, Anne. *The Apprentice of Florence* (1934)
Langton, Jane. *The Fledgling* (1981)
Larson, Kirby. *Hattie Big Sky* (2007)
Lasky, Kathryn. *Sugaring Time* (1984)
Latham, Jean Lee. *Carry On, Mr. Bowditch* (1956)
Lathrop, Dorothy P. *The Fairy Circus* (1932)
Lauber, Patricia. *Volcano: The Eruption and Healing of Mount St. Helens* (1987)
Law, Ingrid. *Savvy* (2009)
Lawson, Robert. *The Great Wheel* (1958)
    Rabbit Hill (1945)
Le Guin, Ursula K. *The Tombs of Atuan* (1972)
L'Engle, Madeleine. *A Ring of Endless Light* (1981)
    A Wrinkle in Time (1963)
Lenski, Lois. *Indian Captive: The Story of Mary Jemison* (1942)
    Phebe Fairchild: Her Book (1937)
    Strawberry Girl (1946)
Leodhas, Sorche Nic. *Thistle and Thyme: Tales and Legends from Scotland* (1963)
Lester, Julius. *To Be a Slave* (1969)
Levine, Gail Carson. *Ella Enchanted* (1998)
Lewis, Elizabeth Foreman. *Young Fu of the Upper Yangtze* (1933)
Lide, Alice, and Margaret Johansen. *Ood-Le-Uk the Wanderer* (1931)

Linquist, Jennie. *The Golden Name Day* (1956)

Lisle, Janet Taylor. *Afternoon of the Elves* (1990)

Lobel, Arnold. *Frog and Toad Together* (1973)

Lofting, Hugh. *The Voyages of Doctor Dolittle* (1923)

Lord, Cynthia. *Rules* (2007)

Lownsbery, Eloise. *Out of the Flame* (1932)

Lowry, Lois. *The Giver* (1994)
  Number the Stars (1990)

MacLachlan, Patricia. *Sarah, Plain and Tall* (1986)

Malkus, Alida. *The Dark Star of Itza: The Story of a Pagan Princess* (1931)

Marshall, Bernard. *Cedric, the Forester* (1922)

Martin, Ann M. *A Corner of the Universe* (2003)

Mathis, Sharon Bell. *The Hundred Penny Box* (1976)

Maxwell, William. *The Heavenly Tenants* (1947)

Mazer, Norma Fox. *After the Rain* (1988)

McGraw, Eloise Jarvis. *The Golden Goblet* (1962)
  Moccasin Trail (1953)
  The Moorchild (1997)

McKinley, Robin. *The Blue Sword* (1983)
  The Hero and the Crown (1985)

McKissack, Patricia C. *The Dark-Thirty: Southern Tales of the Supernatural* (1993)

McNeely, Marian Hurd. *The Jumping-Off Place* (1930)

Meader, Stephen W. *Boy with a Pack* (1940)

Means, Florence Crannell. *The Moved-Outers* (1946)

Meigs, Cornelia. *Clearing Weather* (1929)
  Invincible Louisa: The Story of the Author of Little Women (1934)
  Swift Rivers (1933)
  The Windy Hill (1922)

Miles, Miska. *Annie and the Old One* (1972)

Miller, Elizabeth. *Pran of Albania* (1930)

Montgomery, Rutherford. *Kildee House* (1950)

Moon, Grace Purdie. *The Runaway Papoose* (1929)

Moore, Anne Carroll. *Nicholas: A Manhattan Christmas Story* (1925)

Moore, Janet. *The Many Ways of Seeing: An Introduction to the Pleasures of Art* (1970)

Mukerji, Dhan Gopal. *Gay-Neck: The Story of a Pigeon* (1928)

Murphy, Jim. *An American Plague: The True and Terrifying Story of the Yellow Fever Epidemic of 1793* (2004)

    The Great Fire (1996)

Myers, Walter Dean. *Scorpions* (1989)

    Somewhere in the Darkness (1993)

Naylor, Phyllis Reynolds. *Shiloh* (1992)

Nelson, Marilyn. *Carver: A Life in Poems* (2002)

Neville, Emily. *It's Like This, Cat* (1964)

North, Sterling. *Rascal: A Memoir of a Better Era* (1964)

O'Brien, Robert C. *Mrs. Frisby and the Rats of NIMH* (1972)

O'Dell, Scott. *The Black Pearl* (1968)

    Island of the Blue Dolphins (1961)

    The King's Fifth (1967)

    Sing Down the Moon (1971)

Park, Linda Sue. *A Single Shard* (2002)

Parrish, Anne. *The Dream Coach* (1925)

    Floating Island (1931)

    The Story of Appleby Capple (1951)

Paterson, Katherine. *Bridge to Terabithia* (1978)

    The Great Gilly Hopkins (1979)

    Jacob Have I Loved (1981)

Patron, Susan. *The Higher Power of Lucky* (2007)

Paulsen, Gary. *Dogsong* (1986)

    Hatchet (1988)

    The Winter Room (1990)

Peck, Richard. *A Long Way from Chicago* (1999)

    A Year Down Yonder (2001)

Perkins, Lynne Rae. *Criss Cross* (2006)

Pope, Elizabeth Marie. *The Perilous Gard* (1975)

Rankin, Louise. *Daughter of the Mountains* (1949)

Raskin, Ellen. *Figgs & Phantoms* (1975)

    The Westing Game (1979)

Rawlings, Marjorie Kinnan. *The Secret River* (1956)

Rhoads, Dorothy. *The Corn Grows Ripe* (1957)

Robinson, Mabel. *Bright Island* (1938)
    Runner of the Mountain Tops: The Life of Louis Agassiz (1940)
Rourke, Constance. *Audubon* (1937)
    Davy Crockett (1935)
Rylant, Cynthia. *A Fine White Dust* (1987)
    Missing May (1993)
Sachar, Louis. *Holes* (1999)
Sandoz, Mari. *The Horsecatcher* (1958)
Sauer, Julia. *Fog Magic* (1944)
    The Light at Tern Rock (1952)
Sawyer, Ruth. *Roller Skates* (1937)
Schaefer, Jack. *Old Ramon* (1961)
Schlitz, Laura Amy. *Good Masters! Sweet Ladies! Voices from a Medieval Village* (2008)
Schmidt, Gary D. *Lizzie Bright and the Buckminster Boy* (2005)
    The Wednesday Wars (2008)
Schmidt, Sarah. *New Land* (1934)
Seeger, Elizabeth. *The Pageant of Chinese History* (1935)
Selden, George. *The Cricket in Times Square* (1961)
Seredy, Kate. *The Good Master* (1936)
    The Singing Tree (1940)
    The White Stag (1938)
Shannon, Monica. *Dobry* (1935)
Shippen, Katherine. *Men, Microscopes and Living Things* (1956)
    New Found World (1946)
Siegal, Aranka. *Upon the Head of a Goat: A Childhood in Hungary 1939–1944* (1982)
Singer, Isaac Bashevis. *Fearsome Inn* (1968)
    When Shlemiel Went to Warsaw and Other Stories (1969)
    Zlateh the Goat and Other Stories (1967)
Singmaster, Elsie. *Swords of Steel: The Story of a Gettysburg Boy* (1934)
Snedeker, Caroline. *Downright Dencey* (1928)
    The Forgotten Daughter (1934)
Snyder, Zilpha Keatley. *The Egypt Game* (1968)
    The Headless Cupid (1972)
    The Witches of Worm (1973)

Sorensen, Virginia. *Miracles on Maple Hill* (1957)
Speare, Elizabeth George. *The Bronze Bow* (1962)
    The Sign of the Beaver (1984)
    The Witch of Blackbird Pond (1959)
Sperry, Armstrong. *All Sail Set: A Romance of the* Flying Cloud (1936)
    Call It Courage (1941)
Spinelli, Jerry. *Maniac Magee* (1991)
    Wringer (1998)
Staples, Suzanne Fisher. *Shabanu, Daughter of the Wind* (1990)
Steele, Mary Q. *Journey Outside* (1970)
Steele, William O. *The Perilous Road* (1959)
Steig, William. *Abel's Island* (1977)
    Doctor DeSoto (1983)
Stolz, Mary. *Belling the Tiger* (1962)
    The Noonday Friends (1966)
Stong, Phil. *Honk, the Moose* (1936)
Swift, Hildegarde. *Little Blacknose: The Story of a Pioneer* (1930)
    The Railroad to Freedom: A Story of the Civil War (1933)
Taylor, Mildred D. *Roll of Thunder, Hear My Cry* (1977)
Tietjens, Eunice. *Boy of the South Seas* (1932)
Tolan, Stephanie S. *Surviving the Applewhites* (2003)
Treffinger, Carolyn. *Li Lun, Lad of Courage* (1948)
Tunis, Edwin. *Frontier Living* (1962)
Turner, Megan Whalen. *The Thief* (1997)
Ullman, James. *Banner in the Sky* (1955)
van Loon, Hendrik Willem. *The Story of Mankind* (1922)
Voigt, Cynthia. *Dicey's Song* (1983)
    A Solitary Blue (1984)
von Stockum, Hilda. *A Day on Skates: The Story of a Dutch Picnic* (1935)
Weik, Mary H. *The Jazz Man* (1967)
Weil, Ann. *Red Sails to Capri* (1953)
Weiss, Johanna. *The Upstairs Room* (1973)
Weston, Christine. *Bhimsa the Dancing Bear* (1946)
White, E. B. *Charlotte's Web* (1953)
White, Ruth. *Belle Prater's Boy* (1997)

Whitney, Elinor. *Tod of the Fens* (1929)
Wier, Ester. *The Loner* (1964)
Wilder, Laura Ingalls. *By the Shores of Silver Lake* (1940)
  Little Town on the Prairie (1942)
  The Long Winter (1941)
  On the Banks of Plum Creek (1938)
  These Happy Golden Years (1944)
Willard, Nancy. *A Visit to William Blake's Inn: Poems for Innocent and Experienced Travelers* (1982)
Wojciechowska, Maia. *Shadow of a Bull* (1965)
Woodson, Jacqueline. *After Tupac and D Foster* (2009)
  Feathers (2008)
  Show Way (2006)
Yates, Elizabeth. *Amos Fortune, Free Man* (1951)
  Mountain Born (1944)
Yep, Laurence. *Dragon's Gate* (1994)
  Dragonwings (1976)
Young, Ella. *The Tangle-Coated Horse and Other Tales: Episodes from the Fionn Saga* (1930)
  The Wonder Smith and His Son: A Tale from the Golden Childhood of the World (1928)

Newbery Title List

* indicates Newbery winners. All other titles were honor books for the year indicated.

The ABC Bunny. Wanda Gag (1934)
Abel's Island. William Steig (1977)
Abraham Lincoln, Friend of the People. Clara Ingram Judson (1951)
Abraham Lincoln's World. Genevieve Foster (1945)
Across Five Aprils. Irene Hunt (1965)
Adam of the Road. Elizabeth Janet Gray (1943)*
After the Rain. Norma Fox Mazer (1988)
After Tupac and D Foster. Jacqueline Woodson (2009)
Afternoon of the Elves. Janet Taylor Lisle (1990)
Al Capone Does My Shirts. Gennifer Choldenko (2005)
All Alone. Claire Huchet Bishop (1954)
All Sail Set: A Romance of the Flying Cloud. Armstrong Sperry (1936)
Along Came a Dog. Meindert DeJong (1959)
America Is Born: A History for Peter. Gerald W. Johnson (1960)
America Moves Forward: A History for Peter. Gerald W. Johnson (1961)
An American Plague: The True and Terrifying Story of the Yellow Fever Epidemic of 1793. Jim Murphy (2004)
Americans Before Columbus. Elizabeth Baity (1952)

Amos Fortune, Free Man. Elizabeth Yates (1951)*
. . . And Now Miguel. Joseph Krumgold (1954)*
The Animal Family. Randall Jarrell (1966)
Annie and the Old One. Miska Miles (1972)
Anpao: An American Indian Odyssey. Jamake Highwater (1978)
The Apple and the Arrow. Mary and Conrad Buff (1952)
The Apprentice of Florence. Anne Kyle (1934)
Audubon. Constance Rourke (1937)
The Avion My Uncle Flew. Cyrus Fisher (1947)
Banner in the Sky. James Ullman (1955)
The Bears on Hemlock Mountain. Alice Dalgliesh (1953)
Because of Winn-Dixie. Kate DiCamillo (2001)
Belle Prater's Boy. Ruth White (1997)
Belling the Tiger. Mary Stolz (1962)
Better Known as Johnny Appleseed. Mabel Leigh Hunt (1951)
Bhimsa the Dancing Bear. Christine Weston (1946)
Big Tree. Mary and Conrad Buff (1947)
Big Tree of Bunlahy: Stories of My Own Countryside. Padraic Colum
    (1934)
Birthdays of Freedom, Volume I. Genevieve Foster (1953)
The Black Cauldron. Lloyd Alexander (1966)
The Black Fox of Lorne. Marguerite de Angeli (1957)
The Black Pearl. Scott O'Dell (1968)
The Blue Cat of Castle Town. Catherine Coblentz (1950)
The Blue Sword. Robin McKinley (1983)
Blue Willow. Doris Gates (1941)
Boy of the South Seas. Eunice Tietjens (1932)
The Boy Who Was. Grace Hallock (1929)
Boy with a Pack. Stephen W. Meader (1940)
Bridge to Terabithia. Katherine Paterson (1978)*
Bright Island. Mabel Robinson (1938)
The Bronze Bow. Elizabeth George Speare (1962)*
Bud, Not Buddy. Christopher Paul Curtis (2000)*
By the Shores of Silver Lake. Laura Ingalls Wilder (1940)
Caddie Woodlawn. Carol Ryrie Brink (1936)*
Calico Bush. Rachel Field (1932)
Call It Courage. Armstrong Sperry (1941)*

Carry On, Mr. Bowditch. Jean Lee Latham (1956)*
Carver: A Life in Poems. Marilyn Nelson (2002)
The Cat Who Went to Heaven. Elizabeth Coatsworth (1931)*
Catherine, Called Birdy. Karen Cushman (1995)
Cedric, the Forester. Bernard Marshall (1922)
Charlotte's Web. E. B. White (1953)
Children of the Soil: A Story of Scandinavia. Nora Burglon (1933)
Chucaro: Wild Pony of the Pampa. Francis Kalnay (1959)
Clearing Weather. Cornelia Meigs (1929)
The Codfish Musket. Agnes Hewes (1937)
Commodore Perry in the Land of the Shogun. Rhoda Blumberg (1986)
The Corn Grows Ripe. Dorothy Rhoads (1957)
A Corner of the Universe. Ann M. Martin (2003)
The Courage of Sarah Noble. Alice Dalgliesh (1955)
The Cow-Tail Switch and Other West African Stories. Harold Courlander (1948)
Crazy Lady! Jane Leslie Conly (1994)
The Cricket in Times Square. George Selden (1961)
Crispin: The Cross of Lead. Avi (2003)*
Criss Cross. Lynne Rae Perkins (2006)*
Daniel Boone. James Daugherty (1940)*
The Dark Frigate. Charles Boardman Hawes (1924)*
The Dark Is Rising. Susan Cooper (1974)
The Dark Star of Itza: The Story of a Pagan Princess. Alida Malkus (1931)
The Dark-Thirty: Southern Tales of the Supernatural. Patricia C. McKissack (1993)
Daughter of the Mountains. Louise Rankin (1949)
Daughter of the Seine: The Life of Madame Roland. Jeanette Eaton (1930)
Davy Crockett. Constance Rourke (1935)
A Day on Skates: The Story of a Dutch Picnic. Hilda von Stockum (1935)
Dear Mr. Henshaw. Beverly Cleary (1984)*
The Defender. Nicholas Kalashnikoff (1952)
Dicey's Song. Cynthia Voigt (1983)*

Dobry. Monica Shannon (1935)*
Doctor DeSoto. William Steig (1983)
Dogsong. Gary Paulsen (1986)
The Door in the Wall. Marguerite de Angeli (1950)*
Down Ryton Water. Eva Roe Gaggin (1942)
Downright Dencey. Caroline Snedeker 1928
Dragon's Gate. Laurence Yep (1994)
Dragonwings. Laurence Yep (1976)
The Dream Coach. Anne Parrish (1925)
The Ear, the Eye, and the Arm. Nancy Farmer (1995)
The Egypt Game. Zilpha Keatley Snyder (1968)
Eleanor Roosevelt: A Life of Discovery. Russell Freedman (1994)
Elijah of Buxton. Christopher Paul Curtis (2008)
Ella Enchanted. Gail Carson Levine (1998)
Enchantress from the Stars. Sylvia Louise Engdahl (1971)
Everything on a Waffle. Polly Horvath (2002)
The Fairy Circus. Dorothy P. Lathrop (1932)
The Family under the Bridge. Natalie Savage Carlson (1959)
Fearsome Inn. Isaac Bashevis Singer (1968)
Feathers. Jacqueline Woodson (2008)
Figgs & Phantoms. Ellen Raskin (1975)
A Fine White Dust. Cynthia Rylant (1987)
The Fledgling. Jane Langton (1981)
Floating Island. Anne Parrish (1931)
Fog Magic. Julia Sauer (1944)
The Forgotten Daughter. Caroline Snedeker (1934)
Frog and Toad Together. Arnold Lobel (1973)
From the Mixed-Up Files of Mrs. Basil E. Frankweiler. E. L. Konigsburg (1968)*
Frontier Living. Edwin Tunis (1962)
The Gammage Cup. Carol Kendall (1960)
Gandhi, Fighter without a Sword. Jeanette Eaton (1951)
Garram the Hunter: A Boy of the Hill Tribes. Herbert Best (1931)
A Gathering of Days: A New England Girl's Journal, 1830–1832. Joan W. Blos (1980)*
Gay-Neck: The Story of a Pigeon. Dhan Gopal Mukerji (1928)*
George Washington. Genevieve Foster (1950)

George Washington's World. Genevieve Foster (1942)
Getting Near to Baby. Audrey Couloumbis (2000)
Ginger Pye. Eleanor Estes (1952)*
A Girl Named Disaster. Nancy Farmer (1997)
The Giver. Lois Lowry (1994)*
Glory of the Seas. Agnes Hewes (1934)
The Golden Basket. Ludwig Bemelmans (1937)
The Golden Fleece and the Heroes Who Lived Before Achilles. Padraic Colum (1922)
The Golden Goblet. Eloise Jarvis McGraw (1962)
The Golden Name Day. Jennie Linquist (1956)
Gone-Away Lake. Elizabeth Enright (1958)
The Good Master. Kate Seredy (1936)
Good Masters! Sweet Ladies! Voices from a Medieval Village. Laura Amy Schlitz (2008)*
Graven Images. Paul Fleischman (1983)
The Graveyard Book. Neil Gaiman (2009)*
The Great Fire. Jim Murphy (1996)
The Great Gilly Hopkins. Katherine Paterson (1979)
The Great Quest: A Romance of 1826. Charles Boardman Hawes (1922)
The Great Wheel. Robert Lawson (1958)
The Grey King. Susan Cooper (1976)*
Hatchet. Gary Paulsen (1988)
Hattie Big Sky. Kirby Larson (2007)
Have You Seen Tom Thumb? Mabel Leigh Hunt (1943)
The Headless Cupid. Zilpha Keatley Snyder (1972)
The Heavenly Tenants. William Maxwell (1947)
Hello the Boat! Phyllis Crawford (1939)
The Hero and the Crown. Robin McKinley (1985)*
The Hidden Treasure of Glaston. Eleanore Jewett (1947)
The High King. Lloyd Alexander (1969)*
The Higher Power of Lucky. Susan Patron (2007)*
Hitler Youth: Growing Up in Hitler's Shadow. Susan Campbell Bartoletti (2006)
Hitty, Her First Hundred Years. Rachel Field (1930)*
Holes. Louis Sachar (1999)*

Homesick: My Own Story. Jean Fritz (1983)
Honk, the Moose. Phil Stong (1936)
Hoot. Carl Hiaasen (2003)
Hope Was Here. Joan Bauer (2001)
The Horsecatcher. Mari Sandoz (1958)
The House of the Scorpion. Nancy Farmer (2003)
The House of Sixty Fathers. Meindert DeJong (1957)
The Hundred Dresses. Eleanor Estes (1945)
The Hundred Penny Box. Sharon Bell Mathis (1976)
Hurry Home, Candy. Meindert DeJong (1954)
I, Juan de Pareja. Elizabeth Borton de Trevino (1966)*
In the Beginning: Creation Stories from Around the World. Virginia
    Hamilton (1989)
Incident at Hawk's Hill. Allan W. Eckert (1972)
Indian Captive: The Story of Mary Jemison. Lois Lenski (1942)
Invincible Louisa: The Story of the Author of Little Women. Corne-
    lia Meigs (1934)*
Island of the Blue Dolphins. Scott O'Dell (1961)*
It's Like This, Cat. Emily Neville (1964)*
Jacob Have I Loved. Katherine Paterson (1981)*
Jane's Island. Marjorie Allee (1932)
The Jazz Man. Mary H. Weik (1967)
Jennifer, Hecate, Macbeth, William McKinley, and Me, Elizabeth.
    E. L. Konigsburg (1968)
Joey Pigza Loses Control. Jack Gantos (2001)
Johnny Tremain. Esther Forbes (1944)*
Journey Outside. Mary Q. Steele (1970)
Joyful Noise: Poems for Two Voices. Paul Fleischman (1989)*
Julie of the Wolves. Jean Craighead George (1973)*
The Jumping-Off Place. Marian Hurd McNeely (1930)
Justin Morgan Had a Horse. Marguerite Henry (1946)
Kildee House. Rutherford Montgomery (1950)
King of the Wind. Marguerite Henry (1949)*
The King's Fifth. Scott O'Dell (1967)
Kira-Kira. Cynthia Kadohata (2005)*
Kneeknock Rise. Natalie Babbitt (1971)

Leader by Destiny: George Washington, Man and Patriot. Jeanette
    Eaton (1939)
Li Lun, Lad of Courage. Carolyn Treffinger (1948)
The Light at Tern Rock. Julia Sauer (1952)
Like Jake and Me. Mavis Jukes (1985)
Lily's Crossing. Patricia Reilly Giff (1998)
Lincoln: A Photobiography. Russell Freedman (1988)*
Little Blacknose: The Story of a Pioneer. Hildegarde Swift (1930)
Little Town on the Prairie. Laura Ingalls Wilder (1942)
Lizzie Bright and the Buckminster Boy. Gary D. Schmidt (2005)
Lone Journey: The Life of Roger Williams. Jeanette Eaton (1945)
The Loner. Ester Wier (1964)
A Long Way from Chicago. Richard Peck (1999)
The Long Winter. Laura Ingalls Wilder (1941)
Magic Maize. Mary and Conrad Buff (1954)
Maniac Magee. Jerry Spinelli (1991)*
The Many Ways of Seeing: An Introduction to the Pleasures of Art.
    Janet Moore (1970)
The Matchlock Gun. Walter D. Edmonds (1942)*
M. C. Higgins the Great. Virginia Hamilton (1975)*
Meggy MacIntosh. Elizabeth Janet Gray (1931)
Men of Athens. Olivia Coolidge (1963)
Men, Microscopes and Living Things. Katherine Shippen (1956)
The Middle Moffat. Eleanor Estes (1943)
The Midwife's Apprentice. Karen Cushman (1996)*
Millions of Cats. Wanda Gag (1929)
Minn of the Mississippi. Holling C. Holling (1952)
Miracles on Maple Hill. Virginia Sorensen (1957)*
Miss Hickory. Carolyn Sherwin Bailey (1947)*
Missing May. Cynthia Rylant (1993)*
Misty of Chincoteague. Marguerite Henry (1948)
Moccasin Trail. Eloise Jarvis McGraw (1953)
The Moorchild. Eloise Jarvis McGraw (1997)
Mountain Born. Elizabeth Yates (1944)
Mountains Are Free. Julia Davis (1931)
The Moved-Outers. Florence Crannell Means (1946)

The Moves Make the Man. Bruce Brooks (1985)
Mr. Justice Holmes. Clara Ingram Judson (1957)
Mr. Popper's Penguins. Richard and Florence Atwater (1939)
Mrs. Frisby and the Rats of NIMH. Robert C. O'Brien (1972)*
My Brother Sam Is Dead. James Lincoln and Christopher Collier (1975)
My Father's Dragon. Ruth S. Gannett (1949)
My Side of the Mountain. Jean Craighead George (1960)
Nansen. Anna Gertrude Hall (1941)
New Found World. Katherine Shippen (1946)
New Land. Sarah Schmidt (1934)
Nicholas: A Manhattan Christmas Story. Anne Carroll Moore (1925)
Nino. Valenti Angelo (1939)
The Noonday Friends. Mary Stolz (1966)
Nothing But the Truth: A Documentary Novel. Avi (1992)
Number the Stars. Lois Lowry (1990)*
Old Ramon. Jack Schaefer (1961)
The Old Tobacco Shop: A True Account of What Befell a Little Boy in Search of Adventure. William Bowen (1922)
Old Yeller. Fred Gipson (1957)
Olive's Ocean. Kevin Henkes (2004)
On the Banks of Plum Creek. Laura Ingalls Wilder (1938)
On My Honor. Marion Dane Bauer (1987)
The One-Eyed Cat. Paula Fox (1985)
Onion John. Joseph Krumgold (1960)*
Ood-Le-Uk the Wanderer. Alice Lide and Margaret Johansen (1931)
Our Eddie. Sulamith Ish-Kishor (1970)
Our Only May Amelia. Jennifer L. Holm (2000)
Out of the Dust. Karen Hesse (1998)*
Out of the Flame. Eloise Lownsbery (1932)
The Pageant of Chinese History. Elizabeth Seeger (1935)
Pancakes-Paris. Claire Huchet Bishop (1948)
Pecos Bill. James Cloyd Bowman (1938)
Penn. Elizabeth Janet Gray (1939)
Penny from Heaven. Jennifer L. Holm (2007)
The Perilous Gard. Elizabeth Marie Pope (1975)
The Perilous Road. William O. Steele (1959)

Phebe Fairchild: Her Book. Lois Lenski (1937)

Philip Hall Likes Me, I Reckon Maybe. Bette Greene (1975)

Pictures of Hollis Woods. Patricia Reilly Giff (2003)

The Pigtail of Ah Lee Ben Loo, with Seventeen Other Laughable Tales and 200 Comical Silhouettes. John Bennett (1929)

The Planet of Junior Brown. Virginia Hamilton (1972)

Pran of Albania. Elizabeth Miller (1930)

Princess Academy. Shannon Hale (2006)

The Quaint and Curious Quest of Johnny Longfoot. Catherine Besterman (1948)

Queer Person. Ralph Hubbard (1931)

Rabbit Hill. Robert Lawson (1945)*

The Railroad to Freedom: A Story of the Civil War. Hildegarde Swift (1933)

Ramona and Her Father. Beverly Cleary (1978)

Ramona Quimby, Age 8. Beverly Cleary (1982)

Rascal: A Memoir of a Better Era. Sterling North (1964)

Red Sails to Capri. Ann Weil (1953)

Rifles for Watie. Harold V. Keith (1958)*

A Ring of Endless Light. Madeleine L'Engle (1981)

The Road from Home: The Story of an Armenian Girl. David Kherdian (1980)

Roll of Thunder, Hear My Cry. Mildred D. Taylor (1977)*

Roller Skates. Ruth Sawyer (1937)*

Rufus M. Eleanor Estes (1944)

Rules. Cynthia Lord (2007)

The Runaway Papoose. Grace Purdie Moon (1929)

Runner of the Mountain Tops: The Life of Louis Agassiz. Mabel Robinson (1940)

Sarah, Plain and Tall. Patricia MacLachlan (1986)*

Savvy. Ingrid Law (2009)

Scorpions. Walter Dean Myers (1989)

Seabird. Holling C. Holling (1949)

Secret of the Andes. Ann Nolan Clark (1953)*

The Secret River. Marjorie Kinnan Rawlings (1956)

Shabanu, Daughter of the Wind. Suzanne Fisher Staples (1990)

Shadow of a Bull. Maia Wojciechowska (1965)*

Shadrach. Meindert DeJong (1954)
Shen of the Sea. Arthur Bowie Chrisman (1926)*
Shiloh. Phyllis Reynolds Naylor (1992)*
Show Way. Jacqueline Woodson (2006)
The Sign of the Beaver. Elizabeth George Speare (1984)
The Silver Pencil. Alice Dalgliesh (1945)
Sing Down the Moon. Scott O'Dell (1971)
The Singing Tree. Kate Seredy (1940)
A Single Shard. Linda Sue Park (2002)*
The Slave Dancer. Paula Fox (1974)*
Smoky the Cowhorse. Will James (1927)*
A Solitary Blue. Cynthia Voigt (1984)
Somewhere in the Darkness. Walter Dean Myers (1993)
Song of the Pines: A Story of Norwegian Lumbering in Wisconsin.
    Walter and Marion Havighurst (1950)
Sounder. William H. Armstrong (1970)*
Spice and the Devil's Cave. Agnes Hewes (1931)
The Story of Appleby Capple. Anne Parrish (1951)
The Story of Mankind. Hendrik Willem van Loon (1922)*
Story of the Negro. Arna Bontemps (1949)
Strawberry Girl. Lois Lenski (1946)*
A String in the Harp. Nancy Bond (1977)
Sugaring Time. Kathryn Lasky (1984)
The Summer of the Swans. Betsy Byars (1971)*
The Surrender Tree: Poems of Cuba's Struggle for Freedom. Marga-
    rita Engle (2009)
Surviving the Applewhites. Stephanie S. Tolan (2003)
Sweet Whispers, Brother Rush. Virginia Hamilton (1983)
Swift Rivers. Cornelia Meigs (1933)
Swords of Steel: The Story of a Gettysburg Boy. Elsie Singmaster
    (1934)
*The Tale of Despereaux: Being the Story of a Mouse, a Princess, Some
    Soup, and a Spool of Thread.* Kate DiCamillo (2004)*
Tales from Silver Lands. Charles Finger (1925)*
*The Tangle-Coated Horse and Other Tales: Episodes from the Fionn
    Saga.* Ella Young (1930)
Theodore Roosevelt, Fighting Patriot. Clara Ingram Judson (1954)

These Happy Golden Years. Laura Ingalls Wilder (1944)
The Thief. Megan Whalen Turner (1997)
Thimble Summer. Elizabeth Enright (1939)*
Thistle and Thyme: Tales and Legends from Scotland. Sorche Nic
   Leodhas (1963)
To Be a Slave. Julius Lester (1969)
Tod of the Fens. Elinor Whitney (1929)
Tom Paine, Freedom's Apostle. Leo Gurko (1958)
The Tombs of Atuan. Ursula K. LeGuin (1972)
Tree of Freedom. Rebecca Caudill (1950)
The Truce of the Wolf and Other Tales of Old Italy. Mary Gould
   Davis (1932)
The True Confessions of Charlotte Doyle. Avi (1991)
The Trumpeter of Krakow. Eric P. Kelly (1929)*
The Twenty-One Balloons. William Pene du Bois (1948)*
26 Fairmont Avenue. Tomie DePaola (2000)
Underneath. Kathi Appelt (2009)
Up a Road Slowly. Irene Hunt (1967)*
Upon the Head of a Goat: A Childhood in Hungary 1939–1944.
   Aranka Siegal (1982)
The Upstairs Room. Johanna Weiss (1973)
Vaino, A Boy of New Finland. Julia Davis (1930)
The View from Saturday. E. L. Konigsburg (1997)*
*A Visit to William Blake's Inn: Poems for Innocent and Experienced
   Travelers.* Nancy Willard (1982)*
*The Voice that Challenged a Nation: Marian Anderson and the
   Struggle for Equal Rights.* Russell Freedman (2005)
Volcano: The Eruption and Healing of Mount St. Helens. Patricia
   Lauber (1987)
The Voyages of Doctor Dolittle. Hugh Lofting (1923)*
The Voyagers: Being Legends and Romances of Atlantic Discovery.
   Padraic Colum (1926)
Walk Two Moons. Sharon Creech (1995)*
The Wanderer. Sharon Creech (2001)
Waterless Mountain. Laura Adams Armer (1932)*
The Watsons Go to Birmingham—1963. Christopher Paul Curtis
   (1996)

The Wednesday Wars. Gary D. Schmidt (2008)
The Westing Game. Ellen Raskin (1979)*
What Hearts. Bruce Brooks (1993)
What Jamie Saw. Carolyn Coman (1996)
The Wheel on the School. Meindert DeJong (1955)*
When Shlemiel Went to Warsaw and Other Stories. Isaac Bashevis
   Singer (1969)
The Whipping Boy. Sid Fleischman (1987)*
Whistlers' Van. Idwal Jones (1937)
The White Stag. Kate Seredy (1938)*
Whittington. Alan Armstrong (2006)
The Windy Hill. Cornelia Meigs (1922)
The Winged Girl of Knossos. Erick Berry (1934)
The Winter Room. Gary Paulsen (1990)
Winterbound. Margery Williams Bianco (1937)
The Wish Giver: Three Tales of Coven Tree. Bill Brittain (1984)
The Witch of Blackbird Pond. Elizabeth George Speare (1959)*
The Witches of Worm. Zilpha Keatley Snyder (1973)
*The Wonder Smith and His Son: A Tale from the Golden Childhood
   of the World.* Ella Young (1928)
Wonderful Year. Nancy Barnes (1947)
The Wright Brothers: How They Invented the Airplane. Russell
   Freedman (1992)
Wringer. Jerry Spinelli (1998)
A Wrinkle in Time. Madeleine L'Engle (1963)*
A Year Down Yonder. Richard Peck (2001)*
Yolanda's Genius. Carol Fenner (1996)
Young Fu of the Upper Yangtze. Elizabeth Foreman Lewis (1933)*
Young Mac of Fort Vancouver. Mary Jane Carr (1941)
Young Walter Scott. Elizabeth Janet Gray (1936)
Zlateh the Goat and Other Stories. Isaac Bashevis Singer (1967)

Index

About the Author

IN HER MULTIFACETED CAREER as librarian, lecturer, consultant, writer, and storyteller, **Binnie Tate Wilkin** has always been an advocate for children. She has focused on literary fairness to African American children and other minorities. Her persistent aim has been to provide young people with honest materials that prepare them for life and for a multicultural world. This is evident in her two bibliographies, *Survival Themes in Literature for Children and Young People,* first and second editions published by Scarecrow Press. It was always true of her lectures in major library schools around the nation. This book, *African and African American Images in Newbery Award Winning Titles,* adds to that purpose. She is also the author of *African American Librarians in the Far West: Pioneers and Trailblazers,* published by Scarecrow Press in 2006. Although officially retired, Ms. Wilkin continues professional consulting and storytelling.